The white cockade

A story of adven[illegible]
pursuit, [illegible]
when Joh[illegible]
the Irish r[illegible]
than his ow[illegible]

This is the fi[illegible] of the three books by Alexander Cordell about the adventures of John Regan.

Also in Knight
by Alexander Cordell

Witches' Sabbath
The healing blade

Alexander Cordell

The white cockade

KNIGHT BOOKS

the paperback division of Brockhampton Press

ISBN 0 340 16279 1

This edition first published 1973 by Knight, the paperback division of Brockhampton Press, Leicester.
First published 1970 by Brockhampton Press

Printed and bound in Great Britain
by Richard Clay (The Chaucer Press), Ltd,
Bungay, Suffolk

Who fears to speak of Ninety-Eight?
Who blushes at the name?
When cowards mock at patriots' fate,
Who hangs his head for shame?

Irish ballad of the 1798 Rebellion

For Jocelyn Andrews
who, quite rightly,
loves horses

Contents

1	The mission of the white cockade	9
2	Ambush	12
3	The secret journey	19
4	Agent of the Rebellion	24
5	The English dragoons	33
6	Fight with a patriot	40
7	The informer	49
8	Traitor or patriot?	57
9	Press-ganged!	69
10	The *Sea-Hawk*	75
11	Sea battle	83
12	The face in the corpse-candle	94
13	The men of the blazing cap	103
14	The duel	108
	Historical characters	120

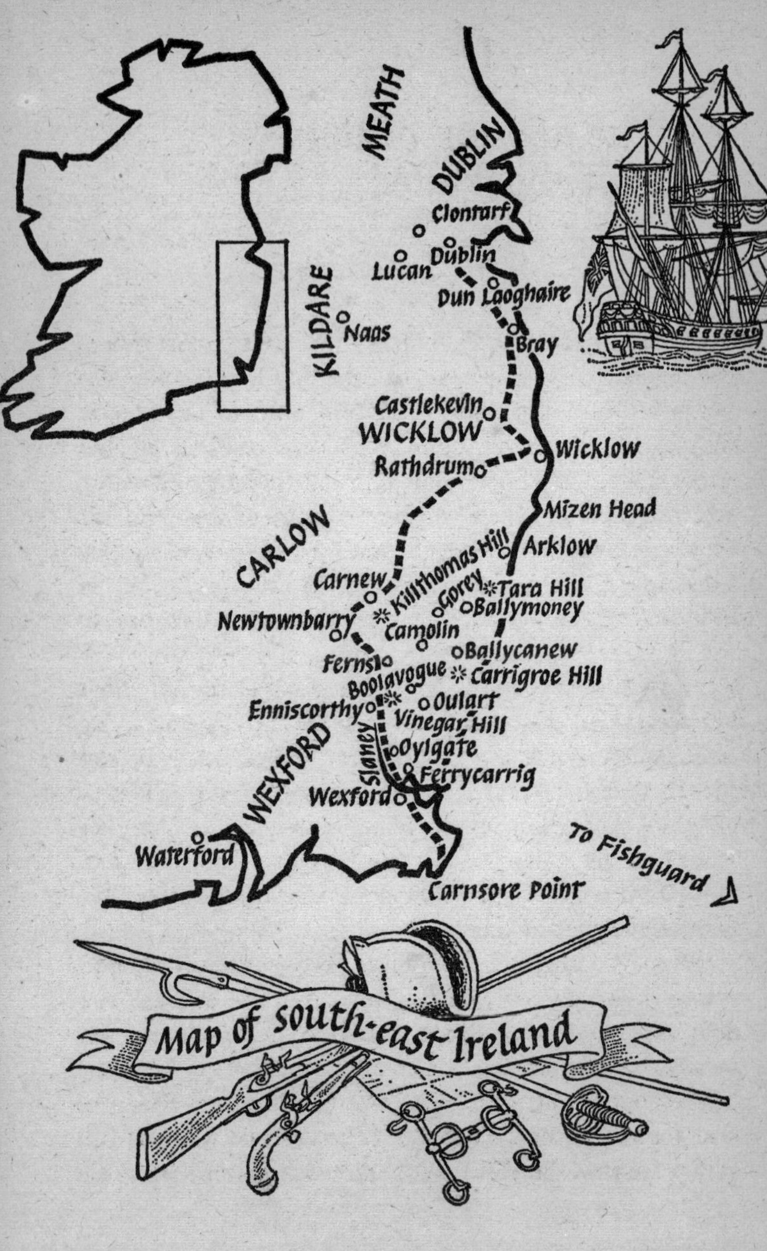
MEATH
DUBLIN
Clontarf
Dublin
Lucan
Dun Laoghaire
KILDARE
Naas
Bray
Castlekevin
WICKLOW
Wicklow
Rathdrum
Mizen Head
CARLOW
Arklow
Killthomas Hill
Carnew
Gorey
Tara Hill
Ballymoney
Newtownbarry
Camolin
Ballycanew
Ferns
Boolavogue
Carrigroe Hill
Enniscorthy
Oulart
Vinegar Hill
WEXFORD
Slaney
Oylgate
Ferrycarrig
Wexford
Waterford
To Fishguard
Carnsore Point
Map of south-east Ireland

1 The mission of the white cockade

THE stars looked so cold that they might faint out of the sky as I took the road to Fishguard, and gave Mia her head. She was a big mare and used to the greater weight of my father, and now she revelled in her strength as if she knew that in us lay the fate of Ireland, and her hooves beat a rhythmic thunder past the tattered hedges all wreathed and ghostly in sea-mist. Breasting a rise I saw the cold, forbidding country of Pembroke stark white under the full May moon, and to the south the estuary lay in crumpled silver, with Nelson's twenty-two ships of the line straining at their hawsers, sails unfurling in the storm like tigers raising their hackles for a new spit at the French. But I did not spare them another glance, and drove on with a billow of white dust rising in the wind blustering in from the wastes of the Atlantic, and the roadside trees were flattened into crippledom, with sand sweeping into my face in little needles of pain.

'Mia, Mia, *Mia* . . .!' I cried above the wind, and reached out, gripping her mane, and she snorted her delight at me, loving this, and tossed the rein, and I felt between my knees the buck and stretch of her, and the heat of her blood, which was one with mine in this mission for my father. Through Johnston we went at full gallop raising the dead with our commotion, with the inn signs creaking for coffin-lids in the storm and the squat houses sitting either side like animals awaiting the spring. On, on to Merlin's Bridge now, and I knew that if they ambushed us for the truth of the white cockade they would do it short of the town: remembering the ambush I loosened the rapier at the hilt and flattened over Mia's neck again, crying to her, and the road that unwound before her flying hooves was a snake of purple under the storm-tossed moon.

After another mile on the gallop, I reined her in and we trotted into a woodland clear of the road. Here a brook was foaming, boasting its way to the sea. Going full length beside Mia, I drank deep, then took off my leather doublet and threw it over her flanks, because she was sweating. And while she rested, grazing, I pulled the little flint-lock pistol from the doublet belt and balled and primed it with the horn, and sat in the shadows of the hedge, watching the road. Soon a coach and four greys came pounding for Milford Haven, and I saw the flash of gold braid, the officers of the line: rolling and bucking, it came, with the horses steaming under the whip and the driver battened down against the wind, the rain swishing from his broad-brimmed hat.

When the coach had passed, I looked at the pistol in my hand, recalling that, not a week ago, my father had touched it. Ambushed on this same road to Fishguard, they had shot him in the back, but Mia had held him and brought him at a trot back home. And when they lifted him from the mare he called for me, no other: he called for me and gave me the letter; the white cockade he gave me, too, before he died. And he bid me die for Ireland also, if I did not deliver the letter.

Now there came to me a great emptiness, and I leaned against a tree. And Mia, sensing my loss, came to me then, with her wet muzzle against my face, as horses do in companionship to those they love. This she often did to my father when he was pleased with her.

I would have wept, then, had Mia not been watching: there are disadvantages, I find, in being grown up, for I was seventeen.

'Away with you, ye skillet,' I said. 'Are we hanging around all day?'

Before I remounted I checked the secret slot in Mia's saddle: the letter for Lord Edward Fitzgerald was still safely there. Putting on my doublet, I adjusted the white cockade at my shoulder. Then I took her on the run, which always delighted her, and she reared up, trying to throw me, pawing the air.

The game was over: flattening her ears she lowered her flanks and we galloped away to the west. The stars were trembling in the storm-swept sky as we raced down the lanes to Fishguard.

For the first time since his death, while Mia could not see, I wept for my father.

2 Ambush

A MILE or so short of Fishguard I reined off the road and took the back lane down to the harbour where the midnight packet was waiting, and I saw her clearly on the emblazoned sea. Almost immediately I felt Mia falter in a scent of danger, and she shrieked, rearing up to a gunpowder flash, and the road became a blaze of incinerating whiteness. In a clatter of hooves I slid from the saddle, rolled into the wayside undergrowth, and lay still: distantly I heard Mia thundering away over the fields, the escape and return my father had taught her. Gripping the hilt of the rapier, I lay there, and I saw, sliding over the ~~stars~~ the heads and shoulders of men and a flash of steel.

'Sure to heaven, we've missed him!'

'Is he away with the horse?'

'He is not, Mike, for I saw him come off. Are ye there, John Regan?'

Motionless, I lay, face in the grass, praying that Mia would return before the hour, as my father had trained her. The tramp of boots came closer; a torch was lighted in a shower of sparks, and it floated along the hedges, turning the night scarlet. Black smoke from the gunpowder flash was lying thick in the hollows and I buried my face in the wetness of the bank, gasping to breathe.

'Are ye there, Regan! You can show yourself, for you've landed among friends.'

I did not move. There were men in Ireland today who claimed the badge of the United Irishmen, but would flog a peasant for the wrong religion and break a man's arm for the price of his silence. This was the scum that had come to the top of the brew; men like the terrible Hessians who carried the torture of the pitch-cap, the picketings, the half-hangings: men who shot in the back.

Now one of them was blundering along the hedge behind me, and, breaking through, I saw him instantly in a drive of the moon; his eyes wide and startled as I leaped up to face him, ducked his lumbering swing, and hooked him square. The meaty smack of fist on bone cracked through their stumbling search. The man sighed and slid against me, and I lowered him to the ground at my feet.

Four of them now.

But the noise of the fight turned them, and they ringed me on the road. Astonishingly, they were unarmed, and one cried, 'It's bound to be the young Regan. He's laid one on Big Tim's whiskers, and he's sleepin' like a child.'

'Keep back,' I said, lifting the rapier.

'Is it true you're young John Regan, lad?' This one was young, with a saucy air on him, all done up in a scarlet doublet and gold earrings.

'No,' I replied.

'Well, whatever your name is, will you put that thing away before somebody gets hurt, for we've little time to spare.'

'What do you want with me?' They approached, their feet shifty on the road, and I backed away to the hedge. The pistol was primed in my pocket, but I dared not reach for it: one careless move, and they would be on me. Distantly I heard Mia galloping. She had been away but a few minutes. Any moment now she might come: she would come at a gallop down the road and slacken so I could mount her. If I was not there she would come again within the hour, as my father had trained her. I had to keep them away until Mia came.

'In the name of heaven,' cried another, 'do we have to break your head before you know an enemy from a patriot. And d'you know something? If we hadn't stopped you here they'd have done so outside Fishguard, and cut your throat from ear to ear.'

'Sure, Patrick, me son, that rhymes!' somebody said, laughing.

'Rhyme it may, but it is God's truth. We're Lord Fitzgerald's men come over special to receive ye, son. Will you put that sword away?'

'Come and get it,' I said.

This was the trouble with Ireland, you couldn't trust your brother. And I did not trust the likes of these, though their brogue was of County Wexford. Yet it was strange that they should come unarmed. I heard one whisper, 'He's a mad Regan, and they breed with tigers. If he carries that sword with the same fever as his father, we'd best break his head and tie him, for there'll be the devil to pay if we're late.'

They came closer, smiling, their hands clenched.

Mia was coming.

My heart began to thud against my shirt. I could hear her plainly. Nearer, nearer she came down the lane from Fishguard, her hooves drumming on the flinted surface. One of the men lifted his bearded face, listening: the unconscious man stirred at my feet. And then, out of the corners of my eyes, I saw Mia. Glistening with sweat and moonlight, she came, her reins dangling free, and foam on her neck. Reaching us, she leaped the road hedge, scattering the men in shrieks, and she wheeled, hooves skidding as I dived for her, gripped her saddle and hauled myself upon her, legs waving. But a man fastened on me from behind, then another, and they heaved me off backwards. I hit the road with a thud and they were instantly upon me. In a welter of hooves and oaths, they pinned me down, and I saw their faces, hard and strong, and the brightness of their eyes. Arching my body, I threw one off, rolled sideways and swung my fist on to the jaw of another clawing after me, but as I scrambled upright three others came, one kicking my legs from under me. Gasping, I lay, and the biggest of them held my throat with one hand and drew back a fist for the blow.

'One move . . .' he gasped. 'One more move, ye mad Regan, an' I'm doin' for ye, d'you get me?'

'Keep your hands off him, Dan!' cried a voice.

'Ach, indeed? And do ye realize he's loosened every tooth in me head?' It was the man I had hit down minutes ago. 'He's got a fist on him like the hoof of a Tipperary mule – did ye see the way he hit me?'

They shouted with laughter at this, and another called, 'And he'll likely hit you again the minute he's up. Are you all right, me son?'

It was the young man of the bangle earrings. Stooping, he pulled the men off and hauled me to my feet while the others gripped me from behind. Fine and reckless he looked standing there with his fists on his hips, and I measured him for size because distantly, in a little flush of wind, I heard Mia's approaching hoofbeats. He cried:

'We apologize for the rough stuff, Regan, but you're not the friendliest of characters yourself.' Bending, he picked up my rapier and gave it to me and the other men freed me. 'Monsieur Poincaré said to take ye, and take you we did. And there's neither bump nor wound on ye, so treat us easy when you report, or we'll be getting the length of his tongue.'

Monsieur Poincaré! There was a magic in the name. This was my father's friend; the Frenchman, probably the finest blade in France, was the link between the coming Rebellion and the most famous names in Paris.

'Your father's friend, me son – do you trust us now?'

'No,' I answered.

'Aye, well trusting or not, you'll be aboard the *Rouen* with your nag and on your way to Ireland in the next ten minutes, and thank your lucky stars for us – French and Irish. For there's twelve men across the road between here and Fishguard – the same who shot your father. You'd have begged for death, man – three are the filthy Hessians.'

This was the terrible regiment brought in by the English; reviled, hated, these mercenary soldiers were the scourge of Ireland.

Mia came trotting up and a man seized her reins, crying:

'The tide's on the turn, Mike. If we don't away now, we'll likely have to swim for it. Has he given the password, for we have our rights, too, remember.'

I smiled at them. It was clean to be among the patriot Irish, and at last I trusted them.

'For God, for honour, for Ireland,' I said.

They ringed me; they pulled back their doublets and showed the white cockade and I turned up the lapel of my tunic and showed them mine, the emblem of my mission.

'For Ireland, the beloved land,' cried one, and they bowed low to me.

They tied muzzle-cloth over Mia's hooves, I noticed, for she was clattering on the rock path to wake the dead as we took a narrow track along the cliff face that led to the sea. And I saw their eyes glittering in their bearded faces, and heard their bass whispers, because they feared the terrible Hessians.

'All right with ye, Regan?' asked one.

'Aye,' I said.

And I gave him a grin. For it was a queer old way, I reflected, of celebrating one's seventeenth birthday – going aboard a French privateer on a voyage to Ireland, under the flag of Poincaré, my father's friend. And with a letter in Mia's saddle for delivery to Lord Edward Fitzgerald, one of the greatest names in Ireland.

Strangely, I knew no fear; only a raking excitement. I had been trained for this. For as long as I could remember, my father had been coming and going between Pembrokeshire and Ireland in the business of organizing this fight to throw off the English yoke. And, like him, I had been born into the service of my country. I knew not the business of geography, but I was trained in the musket and pistol: of arithmetic I knew little, but had learned of the rapier in the French Academy of 1797, where my father was once Principal.

My blood coursed in my veins as I saw the privateer lying on the sea in a sudden rush of the moon, and I longed to be aboard her with Poincaré, the Frenchman, and in service to my beloved Ireland.

But had I known of the blood that would run in the gutters from Meath to Kildare and Wicklow to Wexford, I would have snatched Mia from the hands of the patriots and ridden her back home, and burned the letter to Lord Edward Fitzgerald that held on its page the fate of Ireland.

3 The secret journey

SQUAT and evil looked the *Rouen*: I recognized her instantly as she lay against a derelict wharf east of the harbour, and there was no light on her save a poop-lantern that burned a pool of blood in the ebony waters. Although I had never met Georges Poincaré, my father's link with the Directory in France, I had often seen his little privateer skulking around the Pembrokeshire coast; one moment off St Ann's Head, next tacking impudently into the Haven itself, reporting the movements of the British fleet under Nelson. For the whereabouts of Nelson was important to Ireland. If an Irish rebellion was to be supported by a French landing at Bantry Bay, it was necessary to know where Nelson was at any given time.

Mia, I recall, rolled a white eye at me as a man led her aboard for stabling, and I followed the young Irish patriot to a cabin below decks.

'Monsieur Poincaré – the son of Shaun Regan!'

'Unharmed?' came the reply from within.

'Neither hide nor hair of him, though Dan Furlong's got a loppy jaw on him and Mick Doyle an eye he will not see from for weeks.'

Bellowed laughter as the cabin lock grated. 'You have a Regan fair enough!'

Poincaré swung open the door, his hand out in greeting, his smile wide. He was a big man; of a swarthy countenance, his cheeks were scarred with sword cuts. My father said he was the best agent in France, and rich since birth; being the son of an aristocratic family, it was said that he was the best rapier in Paris, although left-handed, which was unusual. And although I myself had been trained in the Academy of Duelling in Paris, I had never met the man, though his name with the blade was legendary. Many men had fallen to his rapier, my father once told me, but all were killed in honour and all had forced the quarrel. Now a fervent supporter of Napoleon, he had pledged his name to the cause of Ireland. Poincaré indicated a seat opposite his chart desk, and I sat facing him.

He said, 'And now, at last, I meet the son of Shaun Regan, my life-long friend. My regrets, sir, on the death of your father.'

'Why did you bring me here, Monsieur Poincaré?' I asked.

'Because you would have been ambushed outside Fishguard by the enemies of Ireland – did not my crew tell you?' His voice was guttural, yet there was about him a massive charm. He added, 'I save you from the loyalists, and in return you nearly kill my crew!'

'It would have been easier to send a man to meet me in Milford.'

He spread his hands. 'But how could I? There was not time, for you had left already. I was off St Ann's when I learned of your father's death, and that you were acting in his place.'

'How did you know that?'

'It is the business of Poincaré to know all things, my son – that is how I keep my neck. Now then – you wish to be landed in Dublin?'

'I wish to be landed on the coast of Wexford, sir – this was my father's last instruction.'

'But come! This is not good sense. Ninety miles, it is, from Wexford to Dublin. Think of the ride!'

'But I do not wish to go to Dublin, Monsieur Poincaré.'

'Why not? Is not Lord Fitzgerald in Dublin?' He smiled disarmingly. 'Come, John, you are with a friend – is it not true that you have a letter – one given to you by your father for delivery to Fitzgerald?'

'I have no such letter, sir, and I have never heard of this man.'

'So you carry the message in your head?'

I nodded.

'That is a dangerous procedure, young man. And I would not be a dutiful friend if I did not warn you of the extent of the danger.' He came closer to me, bracing his legs to the slant of the floor. For the *Rouen* was under way now, pitching before a stiff easterly wind, and the yellow lights of Fishguard harbour were strung like amber beads across the cabin window. Monsieur Poincaré continued, 'In the coming struggle for Irish freedom my country will join with yours in throwing off the English yoke, but it will not come easily. Traitors are in high places of a corrupt Irish government and in the lowest Irish cabins; spies are everywhere, since the English pay well for information. And men like Carl Labat would burn a man alive for the kind of information you are carrying in your head.'

'Carl Labat?' This mercenary was the terror of Ireland.

Poincaré said, 'Tonight Carl Labat was across the road to Fishguard, waiting for you, but I struck first. You were taken too easily, John. How would it be for you now, if you were standing before the terrible Labat instead of before me, Poincaré?'

I turned away from his searching eyes, realizing the sense of it, and the temptation to share the secret with this capable and clever man nearly overcame me. For if any man in the world could get that letter to Lord Fitzgerald, it was Georges Poincaré. It was said that he had the ear of Hoche, the brilliant young French general: and even the admiration of Bonaparte himself. Now he said, 'See the sense of it, young man. Is it right that the fate of Ireland should hang on the courage of a lad of seventeen? Would your father have given this message to you, had I been near to take it? Come, courage is not enough – share this secret with your father's friend.'

I closed my eyes, turning away. 'I cannot, sir. My father gave it to me and bid me share it with no other.'

'But did he reckon on me, Poincaré?'

I did not reply, and he whispered, 'See the danger, my son. Were I Carl Labat standing here instead of Poincaré, you would talk within the hour.'

I swung to him. 'I would not. He could burn me alive, but I would not!'

'In the last resort, that is probably what would happen – you do not know men like Carl Labat. Now, then?'

'I cannot break my word to my father,' I said, and to my astonishment he smiled, and cried:

'Congratulations! You are indeed your father's son. *Mon Dieu!* Listen! My instructions from the French Director were to trap and test you, before somebody like Labat got the opportunity.' He crossed his heart, adding, 'I pray to God that you never meet this man. Meanwhile, I can report to the French Directory that you have the message and that you will not be found wanting.'

Later, we drank coffee and talked of the coming Irish rebellion. Later still, he showed me to a tiny cabin, and there I rolled into the hammock and prepared to sleep, until I remembered Mia.

It was cold on the rain-swept deck, and the steersman was standing like monumental stone against a storm-crested sea, and the Irish mist was billowing over the hatches. With the wind shrieking in the rigging, I staggered aft, and went below. Mia was stamping in her stall; they had fed and watered her, but she was still saddled, and she snorted her indignation when she saw me in the doorway, for she hated the saddle.

'You'll have to put up with it,' I whispered in her ear.

Strange and eerie, it is, when you know you are being watched but cannot see the eyes.

With the lantern painting a yellow circle at my feet, I went back to the cabin, but I did not sleep. For a name was beating in my brain.

Carl Labat. *Carl Labat.*

4 Agent of the Rebellion

MONSIEUR POINCARÉ brought the *Rouen* close inshore, and his crew planked me ashore to the ruined jetty of Carnsore: over this I led Mia, mounted her and galloped north and across the deserted Wexford Bridge on the road to Enniscorthy, and I did not even turn to wave to the *Rouen,* since there was no time for pleasantries. Icy fangs were in the dawn wind, although it was May and there was a slaughter of blood in the eastern sky. Wexford quay was tomb-quiet as we galloped along, with the ships straining at their hawsers like prehistoric monsters. And I thought of the curragh men from Scandinavia who had settled here from the Atlantic coasts of France and Spain, before the coming of the Faith. And I thought, in the rhythmic beat of Mia's hooves, of the Vikings who came as traders, seeking a base to winter their longships; of Black Tom, the Earl of Ormonde and friend of Queen Elizabeth I, and the dead knights of Fitzstephen the Dane who lay like shrouded ghosts along the road that I was galloping now. It seemed to me that Mia herself scented this battleground of the past, once stained with Danish and Norman blood: a battleground that would soon stain again with the dead of a modern and vicious rebellion.

And then, as I crossed the bridge to Ferrycarrig, I suddenly remembered my father who had taught me this history: in his memory, I reined in, dismounted and led Mia into the shadows of the Promontory Fort. Here I knelt and kissed the soil of the verge, because I was one with my country and my people. I also prayed, first for my mother, who was a Catholic and had died at my birth, and after this prayer I crossed myself: then I prayed for my father, but after this prayer I did not cross myself since he was a Protestant. Mia was watching me with a puzzled expression as I rose to mount her.

With my foot in the stirrup, I heard it: galloping hooves.

Swiftly, I drew Mia into the shadows, and waited.

The hoof-beats ceased.

'Stand!' I whispered, and scrambled up the Fort escarpment. Full length I lay, parting the grass. A horseman was standing beyond the bright sheen of the estuary: clearly, I saw him; a big man, and he sat his horse magnificently, and I could almost hear him listening for the hoof-beats of Mia. And I knew with certainty that the moment we moved again, he would follow.

The bulge of the letter in Mia's saddle was a balm to my touch.

'We'll give him a run for it, girl,' I said. '*Away!*'

The dawn of rebellion was flushing the sky as we took headlong up the road to the north. And I knew that after five miles we had lost him, for there wasn't a mare or horse either side of the Irish sea who could live with Mia, and she knew it.

On, then, to Enniscorthy and Joe Lehane of Rudd's

Inn who was a United Irishman and a friend of the white cockade. Joe Lehane, who had a pretty daughter called Kathleen.

'If he indeed has a daughter called Kathleen,' said my father, 'this will prove that you've got the right Joe Lehane, for there's a couple of dozen of them in the town of Enniscorthy.'

On high ground short of Enniscorthy I rested Mia again for she was coming heavy in the chest with her, and I saw in the distance the jagged mound of the hideous Vinegar Hill stark black against the stars of morning, and to the west a great bonfire was burning in flames of red and gold against the brightening sky. Then I was aware that other fires were blazing, and I scrambled to the top of a rocky mound and looked down over the misted country. Six fires I counted in the Slaney valley, and knew that they were peasant cabins burning, for in a warm flush of the wind I heard the shriek of women and the bass-shouts of men. Aboard the *Rouen* Poincaré had said that the North Cork Militia were in the vicinity searching for arms, and I took this for their work, a regiment hated by the peasantry.

I screwed up my hands to a deep and violent hatred. At first hand, now, I was seeing the things of which my father had spoken. Under the English General Lake the British and their mercenaries ranged the country night and day, searching sheds and barns for evidence of the coming uprising. For the patriot Irish were forging pike-heads in their smithies, and moulding lead shot and canister for the little square cannons. Ammunition was being carried by night from the coast of France and landed in the secret channels of Ireland, there to be buried until the day of the rebellion. And the innocent as well as the guilty were being pulled from their beds and flogged for information, or dragged before a military tribunal, there to be sentenced to transportation, sometimes on mere suspicion. So the country was in a ferment; the brutal treatment brought Irish retaliation. Minor fights were building up between Antrim and Wexford; British soldiers and their mercenaries were found dead in the fields; judges were threatened, informers whipped: women had their hair cut off for consorting with the invaders.

I saw in those burning cabins the misery of my people: from the time of the Beast Cromwell to the invading General Lake my country had known little but agony.

The little town of Enniscorthy was deserted as I galloped to Rudd's Inn. A sleepy ostler took Mia's head as I clattered into the stable yard. The inn was as quiet as an undertaker's parlour; I shivered, staring around.

'I will take the saddle,' I said to the ostler.

With the house asleep, he showed me to an attic room. There I flung myself on the bed, and slept: awaking instantly, it seemed, to bright sunlight filtering through a window. I felt refreshed and strong; the terror of the burning cabins had gone. It was a beautiful May morning.

And standing by my bed was a jovial little fat man with a red, cherubic face and sandy hair.

'Your servant, John Regan,' said he, and bowed. I sat up instantly.

'You know my name?'

'Arrah!' He pulled the curtains wider and the sun streamed in. 'It's the business of the Lehanes to know the comings and goings of important people, you see – especially between Wexford and Dublin.' He rubbed his hands, his expression impish. 'Aye, well, it will not be the first time a man's been recognized by the horse that carries him. And you sleepin' there were the spit and image of the great Shaun Regan of Milford, the United Irishman living in Wales. Has he ever made speak of me, Joe Lehane?'

I did not reply. I was pulling on my trews.

'Don't ye trust me, son?'

'No,' I said.

'And me host to yer dad these past seven years. Shall I give ye the proof of it?' Hands on hips, he grinned the challenge and I followed him down into the stable yard where Mia was under the brush, and he called her name and tossed up a piece of honey and sugar and she snapped it and left the ostler and came to him, nuzzling his face in soft whinnies.

'It's somethin' to be trusted by the horse and not the rider,' said Joe Lehane. Back in my room, he said:

'Is that saddle so sweet and perfumed that you have to sleep wi' it?'

'I keep my money in it,' I said, and flung cold water into my face, and took the towel he tossed me and rubbed for a glow.

'It's a quick answer, me boy, and ye've a lively head,

which is fine. But you'll have to be livelier to find answers to some of the questions you'll be asked round here. Where are ye bound?'

'My business,' I replied.

'O, aye? And mine, too. For if you're the son of Shaun Regan in truth, it's me duty as a United Irishman to help ye on your way, for the place is swarming with Royalists pledged to let your blood. Can ye give me proof, or I might think it safer to hand ye to the filthy Hessians for stealin' Shaun Regan's horse.'

Smiling, I drew back my doublet and showed the white cockade, and he sighed with relief, whispering deep in his throat, 'God bless ye, son, but why isn't your father on this errand of life or death?'

'He is dead, Mr Lehane. They shot him in the back.'

As if in sudden agony, he crossed himself, saying, 'God in heaven! There's more fine men goin' under than on the soles of their feet, I'm thinking. And there'll be thousands more, I'll warrant, before the land is free. Do you need further proof of me, Regan? If so, name it.'

'Call your daughter,' I said.

'Me daughter? What's she to do with it?'

'Call her.'

He called down the stairs, and within a minute a girl entered the room; I judged her as a year younger than me; she had eyes wide and sparkling for me, and a thick brogue from Wexford.

'What is your name?' I asked.

'Sure, if I tell ye that you'll be as wise as me,' said she.

'Tell him your name,' commanded her father.

Her brow clouded and she was pert and very pretty with her. 'Kathleen.'

'Right,' said Joe, 'away wi' ye.' He shut the door behind her. 'Now for the letter, son.'

'I have no letter – the message is in my head.'

'Blood an' hounds! You must have a letter – d'ye think Lord Edward will take the word of a lad of seventeen?'

'He will have to. For I have no letter.'

For a half-hanging, a whip, the screw, the pitch-cap blazing, I would tell no man alive, except Lord Fitzgerald, that I possessed my father's letter.

'Right, then – letter or not, you'll now take the instructions I was to give your father, or the Committee will skin me. *Listen!* The United Irishmen leaders are split all over Dublin, because of security. Lord Edward himself is changing his address from hour to hour. One minute O'Connor and Sweetman are with him, next minute it's Keugh and McCormick or McNevin and Drennan. Do you get me, son?'

'Aye!'

'And Fitzgerald's no fool. One week he's in Bridge Street with Oliver Bond, the printer; next week he's out of Dublin and heaven knows where. The Pimpernel, they call him. Bless me soul to hell – a week last Friday I came into the pot-room with the roast, and there he was as large as life sitting down to dinner.'

'In here?' Incredulous, I stared at him.

'Under this roof – and the Dublin Militia of two-faced Irishmen burning the cabins not half a mile from

Enniscorthy – and him with a thousand English pounds on his head!'

'Some man,' I said.

'Aye,' and Joe Lehane drew himself up, 'some man, and I'll tell ye something – I'd not be in your shoes if you tell that message to anyone but him, for he'd call it treason. Aye, call it treason, he would, even if it was Carl Labat himself who forced it from your teeth.'

'Carl Labat? What do you know of him?' I whispered.

His face drained of its colour and he crossed himself again. 'A captain in a German regiment – I know nothing more.' He gripped my arm. 'But I tell you this, Regan; you'll pray for death if ever you meet him, and like as not you'll find him behind the first door you knock on in Dublin city, if not before.' Sweat beaded his face and he wiped it into his hair, sighing. 'So tell your beads, son, when ye knock on doors in Dublin.'

I got up and walked to the window, staring down at the stable yard. What with one and the other of them, I thought, I'd soon be dreaming of this terrible Carl Labat.

'Downstairs for your breakfast now, son, before the house becomes suspicious.'

As he spoke a big, handsome man led his horse into the yard and saddled it, tightening the girths, and there was a loose-limbed strength about him; a dignity I thought I had seen somewhere before. I said to Joe Lehane:

'Who's the guest?'

Lehane shrugged. 'Man called Barrington – he came

in from Wexford late last night – just after you, I think.'

'Was his horse sweating?'

'Like a Spanish bull – I stabled it meself – he must have been riding hard. Why?'

Without a doubt, this was the man I had seen outside Wexford near the Promontory Fort, and, at the time, believed him to be following me.

5 The English dragoons

I STAYED the daylight hours at Rudd's Inn with Joe Lehane and his daughter, since it was quicker to ride in darkness and arrive in one piece than to be ambushed in daylight and never arrive at all; more, it rested Mia, for she was more the racehorse than the hack, and liked the shorter distances. Also, Redcoat cavalry had entered the town that morning; men of the English counties of Hampshire and Dorsetshire, the élite of General Lake's army, and I admired the way they rode and the fine dignity of them, for these were not the riff-raff mercenaries that England shuffled into Ireland: these were not the men who flogged and burned and looted. There might have been no '98 Rebellion in Ireland had the land been policed by such as these.

But for all my admiration of them my heart nearly stopped when they trooped their great horses into the yard of the inn and tethered them either side of Mia who was waiting saddled, ready for darkness.

'Are ye there, John?' I was in my bedroom when Kathleen knocked, peering through a crack of the curtains down into the stable yard.

'Aye!' Swiftly, I opened the door.

She entered, throwing some rough clothes on to the bed. 'Me father says they'll likely ask questions about the guests, and you're safer as a pot-boy than a passing stranger.'

'Will they fit me?' I asked, holding up the clothes.

'A bit tight around the ears,' she said, 'but a rope would be tighter.'

I got into them and was half-way down the stairs when Joe Lehane shouted:

'Pot-boy!'

'Aye, sir?' I shouted back.

'Down to the cellar with you and bring another hogshead for the English soldiers!'

'This minute, sir.'

And Kathleen was on the cellar steps with me coming up carrying the hogshead of ale, and there was a fine beauty on her, with her hair flowing black to her narrow waist, and I reckoned that if I walked a woman over dream-cloud hill on a Sunday morning it would likely be Kathleen, the daughter of Joe Lehane.

'You'll be coming back from Dublin city in one piece?' she asked.

'If I have a hand in it,' I replied, shifting the hogshead on to the other shoulder.

'And stoppin' here in Enniscorthy, too?'

'Unless they've got prettier tap-maids the other side of the Slaney.'

She smelled of lavender, I remember, as if she had pinned wild sprigs of it in her clothes, and grew it in her hair. Her father bellowed, then:

'Is that hogshead coming, pot-boy, or do I come down there and lift it meself?'

'Coming now, sir!' I shouted back.

But we did not move on the cellar stairs – Kathleen, me and the hogshead, and she said, of a sudden:

'Will you wear this trinket to keep you safe, John Regan?' and she brought from her pocket a little St Christopher medallion, and put it around my neck. 'And I will pray for you.'

'Pray for Ireland, Kathleen.'

'I will that – for the pair of you, for you're one an' the same.'

We stood apart, just looking, mainly at the floor, for there was a mile between us in this business of life or death. Then she said:

'Now you'd best get that hogshead up to my dad, or you'll never hear the end of it.' She began to giggle then, as I climbed the steps, with her hands clapped over her mouth and red in the face with her.

'What's up?' I asked, looking back.

'The last pot-boy was five foot high,' she said, 'so your waistcoat's splittin' and your trews are half-way up your legs.'

I left her collapsed on the steps rocking with laughter, but there was nothing to laugh about when I reached the tap-room.

The eyes of the soldiers switched to me as I carried in the hogshead, and for a fleeting moment I was sure Mr Lehane had betrayed me. Nobody moved. With their quart pewters of ale held in their fists, they watched me as I set the cask down behind the tap: seven feet tall they looked in their scarlet tunics and curved brass helmets, the aristocracy of the English army. I wouldn't have tangled with one of them for all the gold in the

Irish mint. I got up behind the tap, and made to leave.

'Wait,' commanded the sergeant.

I waited, stooping, staring at the floor, leaving it to Joe Lehane.

The sergeant said to him, 'So there's you and your daughter: there is the ostler we saw outside, and this one.' He nodded towards me.

'That's the lot,' said the landlord, and I admired his nerve. In Ireland, at this time, it was your ability at lying that saved your neck or dressed you for your coffin.

'And you've no guests?'

'None save the fella that left us this morning.'

'His name?'

'He said his name was Jonah Barrington.'

The sergeant grunted, drank deep of his quarter and put it on the counter.

'And you – what's your name?' he said to me.

'Tim McCoy,' answered Lehane.

The sergeant swung to him. 'Has he got no tongue of his own?'

'He has,' replied the landlord coolly, 'but you'll get little sense from him because he's not of the brightest – he's only one short of the ostler, and he's plain daft.'

The sergeant came closer, put out his hand and raised my face to his. His eyes, bright blue in his tanned face, burned into mine.

'What's your name, lad?'

'Tim,' I said huskily.

'Tim what?'

'Tim McCoy, sir.'

The room tingled with silence. The door leading to the yard was open, and I saw over the sergeant's shoulder the heather fanning live in the wind on the hills above Enniscorthy, and I saw Mia stamping on the cobbles and fought down the temptation to make a dash for it. For, once astride her they would not catch me, this I knew. But I also knew that to run for it now would put a rope around the neck of Joe Lehane, the patriot.

'He don't look so daft to me,' rumbled the sergeant. 'Where you hail from?'

'Enniscorthy,' I replied.

'And when did you start here?'

'Last Christmas I took him on,' said Joe, and stared at me.

With deliberation, I said to the sergeant, 'He's lying, sir. I come last November.'

Joe cried, 'The boy's half-soaked – I took him on last Christmas Eve . . .'

'It is not important,' said the sergeant.

'It is,' I shouted. 'He's always calling me soaked. I started here last November, when my ma died, and he knows it.'

'I told you he was bats in the belfry, Sergeant,' said Joe, turning away.

I said bitterly, 'I come in November, an' I'm not as daft as he makes out.'

The eyes of the soldiers moved from one to the other of us, weighing the situation. The sergeant drained his pewter and put it on the counter. 'It's all right, son,' he said, and gripped my shoulder. At the door he turned to

Joe. 'You're hard on him, landlord. If you keep treating him like a half-wit he'll end up as one, and that's not Christian.' He glanced at his watch. 'When did this chap Barrington leave?'

'The . . . the guest?' asked Joe.

'The man who stayed the night – you said his name was Barrington.'

'About ten o'clock,' answered Joe Lehane.

The sergeant grunted, and said, turning back, 'You'd best know it, landlord, for you'll swing for sure if you don't give us the truth of it. We're looking for a messenger come from Milford and bound for Dublin. He was put ashore last night at Wexford, and he didn't travel on the Fishguard packet. Now then – have ye seen such a chap, for he was roughly the size and age of this one here.' He thumbed my chest.

'Only Barrington, an' he was inches larger all round, sir,' said Joe.

'And he came in off the Wexford road?'

'He did that.'

A soldier said, 'Sounds like our man, Sergeant.'

'It does not,' replied the sergeant, eyeing me, 'but we'd best go after him.'

To avoid suspicion, I went into the yard with them to help them mount, and my heart nearly stopped when Mia saw me and whinnied her joy at me, but nobody appeared to notice.

It is the odd mistakes like this that hang a man, said Joe later, you rarely hang for the big ones.

They clattered out of the stable yard in a chink of reins and sabres, and we watched their scarlet tunics and flashing helmets bobbing over the hedges along the road to Oulart.

'Thank God they're gone,' said Kathleen, coming up.

'It was a near thing,' said Joe, 'and you missed a fine display of acting.'

6 Fight with a patriot

I LEFT Rudd's Inn at dusk without sending it a backward glance, though I knew that Kathleen was watching from a top window. With a forced casual air I trotted Mia through the market-day crowds thronging down from the castle, and I saw in their eyes a sullen anger at the burning of their cabins, and knew that this was a people ripe for revolution. There was no laughter in them, which is foreign for Irish who are all laughter: gaunt and craggy were the faces of the men as they shepherded their shawled women past the arrogant stares of the soldiers of the Hessians who stood on guard at street corners. Later, I knew that it was these same Irish patriots who, but a few weeks later, drove their cattle against the Enniscorthy garrison in the manner of Strongbow, and spilled their lives on Slaney Bridge and among the crags of Vinegar Hill under the banner of the great Father Murphy, whom they adored.

A black bear was dancing on a chain to the music of an organ-grinder: urchins scuttled among the crowd, pick-pockets moved with loose hands and innocent stares. Ladies in fine crinolines, the women of the foreign officers, walked with grace among the beggars of the walls who flung out their hands for alms. And I knew, with a sudden shock, that the letter I carried in Mia's saddle would spell life or death for every human being there, on that evening in Enniscorthy: that freedom or enslavement for generations unborn would depend on whether or not I got it safely to Dublin. And I knew, too, that many people stood between me and Lord Fitzgerald, who awaited it; that the enemies of Ireland would leave nothing undone to prevent it reaching its destination.

For this was a time of terror for Ireland. The spies of a corrupt government were lying under the floor-boards and sewing their noses to key-holes in search of information. England knew that the Reign of Terror that had bathed France in blood could happen again. On the other side of the English Channel the French fleet was poised to strike at the Irish shore and land an army in support of the patriots: up in Antrim and Down the Irish peasantry was being held on the leash like chained tigers by men like McCracken and Monroe, the draper. And Britain, driven to a new desperation, pillaged and burned and flogged to find the buried arms of the planned rebellion. The pot that had simmered in my country for two centuries since the Barbarian Cromwell now frothed and bubbled, ready to overflow.

It was dark when I galloped Mia through Newtownbarry and nearly midnight when the sleepy little gables of Carnew spiked the western sky. It was a fine night, with a touch of cold in the wind, and the hedges, rimmed with sea-mist, snatched thorny fingers at us as we raced along, and the trees raised threatening arms at the outrage, like bears disturbed at feasting. In a thunder we went, Mia and I, and I shouted to her for company and smoothed her flattened ears.

South of Carnew I reined her off the road and took cross-country, for according to Joe fighting had broken out between the Presbyterians and Catholics, as it had done over ten years back between the Defenders and Peep o' Day Boys, and the militia had been called out and were astride the roads. Yet I saw Carnew later, a town dead under the bright moon. Mia was sweating badly then, I remember, so I trotted her into a forest rise and down the ride to a cave of which Joe had spoken. Tethering the mare at the entrance I went full length, staring up into the sky of candle-flame stars. Before I slept, I primed the little pistol and set it down beside me, knowing that at the first human footstep, Mia would wake me.

I slept.

I dreamed.

I dreamed of a forest clearing and a man sleeping in leaves: arms and legs flung out, he slept in exhaustion, silent, unmoving, like a man dead. And while he slept another moved through the forest, his feet silent in the refuse of autumn, and I saw him clearly, moving through shafts of moonlight towards the sleeping man. In his hand was a stone, and his eyes were bright and glittering in his bearded face, as if with an inner madness. Reaching the sleeper, he paused and lifted the stone. And as he lifted it he screamed at the sky, and the forest echoed to that scream, reverberating and dying in the instant before Mia screamed, as horses do. And the horror of it entered me, making me a part of the dream, and I involuntarily rose, seeing at once the form of a man outlined against the stars. Automatically, I swept the ground for the pistol: it was no longer there.

It was steady in the hand of the man in the entrance.

'Get up,' he said.

I did so.

At first, because of his great size, I thought he was the man who had pursued me from Wexford to Enniscorthy. But then his horse wandered beside Mia, and it was white. I could not see the man's face because it was set against moonlight, but I sensed the strength of him, and, despite his size, there was a litheness in his movements that told me he was young.

'Now then,' he murmured, and his finger tightened on the pistol.

'What do you want of me?'

'Are ye here in the name of the patriots?'

'I am,' I replied.

He laughed, his voice deep. 'That's a good 'un. You leave the table of Bagenal Harvey, ye sup with him and give the hand of friendship. And the moment he turns his back you take horse for Dublin in the name of the Crown.'

'I do not know what you are talking about.'

'D'ye not? God's blood, man, you will before tonight is finished. For I know the truth of you – I tracked you from Bargy Castle to Enniscorthy. And you were there for a meeting of the dragoons from New Ross, and them riding off to Gorey to lay the plans before the Committee.' He came closer. 'In all truth, man, do ye deserve to live when you break bread with gentlemen like Harvey and Keugh, and then take horse to betray them?'

I said evenly, 'You have got the wrong man. I have never heard of the men you speak of, I have never set foot in Bargy Castle, wherever that may be.'

'O, aye, indeed! But I wager ye know Rudd's Inn and Joe Lehane?'

'Yes.'

'Do ye deny you stayed there last night?'

'No. It is true that I stayed there.'

'And had a meeting with the English dragoons?'

'There was no meeting – they came by chance.'

'And where are ye off now, then?'

'To Dublin.'

'Ye don't deny that?' For the first time I noticed his speech was uneducated.

'I do not. I'm for Dublin the moment we're finished talking.'

'You're not going to Dublin, Jonah Barrington; you're heading back to Bargy Castle in Wexford.'

'Wait,' I said, and folded back the leather of my doublet and moved into a shaft of the moon so he could see the white cockade, taking a chance that he might know the emblem.

'What's that thing?' he demanded.

'The white cockade. For God, for honour, for Ireland.'

'Is it, indeed!' He laughed. 'Sure, if it's a patriot man you are, you'd be wearing the green. For the white is the white feather of Jonah Barrington.'

'My name is not Barrington,' I said. 'It is John Regan.'

'You can tell that to Mr Bagenal Harvey when we get back to Bargy Castle,' said he, motioning with my pistol. 'Outside, ye skillet!'

I knew that once he got me outside the cave he would ride behind me the forty miles or so back to Wexford: that all my entreaties that we should call at Rudd's Inn where Joe Lehane and Kathleen would vouch for me would prove of no avail. And there was no doubt, either, that he was mistaking me for the man called Barrington who had stayed at the inn with me on the previous night. Further, while this was an Irish patriot he was doing no good for Ireland by arresting me – if it was this man Barrington he was after, he ought to go after him for the sake of the general cause. I couldn't afford the time to go back to Wexford to satisfy a whim that would end in apologies all round.

'Come on, come on!' he commanded, for I was wasting time in picking up Mia's precious saddle.

And he fired the pistol as I straighted and flung the saddle at his legs. Momentarily, he staggered, and I was upon him like lightning, sinking my right fist deep into his body and catching him with a raging uppercut as he went double, grunting. This flung him back, and he hit the wall of the cave with a thud, and lay there, swaying, his arms loose, fighting for breath. Mia and the big white horse were rearing and stamping as I ran into the moonlight, untethered the white horse and slapped his flank. And as he galloped down the road I threw the saddle across Mia's back and prepared to tighten the girths, but the man was upon me again, ducking under her belly and diving at my legs. Together, we rolled and fought under Mia's stamping hooves: rising, I threw him backwards, and as I rose he clambered up, ready. And shouting hoarsely, he came in hooking to have my head off, but I side-stepped, and he floundered past me, staggered, and turned. And I saw his eyes bright and shining on his square, strong face, and knew him to be at least twice as old as I was. A man of thirty is a bad age to tangle with, for he is built to last. I think I knew that unless I finished the fight almost at once, that he would better me: automatically, my hand dropped to the hilt of the rapier at my belt. I could have again side-stepped his bull-like rush and run him through in passing, but I could not. For all his lumbering passion, he was, like me, an Irish patriot, and I could not even wound him.

'You swine loyalist,' he cried. 'You'll stand before Bagenal Harvey or I die takin' ye!' and came in, fists swinging.

This is the time to take it slow, said my father: this is the moment of coolness. I stood ground, braced my feet, swayed away from his chopping blows and hooked him with every ounce of my strength. The blow took him square. The added impact of his onward charge shuddered through my body. He halted, like a bear pole-axed, and began to turn slowly, his eyes glazed. Without so much as a sigh, he slipped down the front of me and I caught him in my arms and lowered him to the ground.

'Sorry, man,' I said, and loosened his collar. Almost

instantly, he stirred, his body tensing to the fighting spirit deep within him. I knew that if I delayed another minute he would be up and barging about again, for there are men who do not know when they are beaten. Leaping at Mia, I swung myself across her back and galloped through the wood in the filtering light of the moon. And as I went I reined in and caught the bridle of the big white horse and took him with us out of the ride and down the clear white road for two miles towards Tinahely, then loosed him. He took a wild, neighing gallop at once, and beautiful indeed he looked with his mane flying free and his ghostly hooves thudding over the short turf of the moor. And he rose up, prancing at the stars in his marvellous freedom. Suddenly, as if remembering his master, he wheeled and galloped down the road we had come. I knew, then, that five minutes later the Irish patriot would be aboard again and looking for my chin. I had to grin as I licked my swollen hand. Next time, sure as fate, it would be me collecting it, for it was a very lucky blow.

'Right, away!' I spurred Mia hard and we went up that road to Tinahely like a saint after demons, swam the river south of Rathdrum and headed north down the country lanes for the sea.

Now there was a smell of wind and billows in the night and a salt tang biting at my eyes. Pale and lovely were the stars of that dawn, I remember, with Our Father's mansions glorious in the sky, and the moon of heaven preening herself all bare and beautiful upon the tallest spire of Wicklow.

In a little hollow clear of the road I prayed for my father, thankful for my delivery.

For in this hollow by the side of the road to Wicklow, once he and I had rested, and I knew with him a warmth and nearness.

7 The informer

NEAR the hollow was an ancient barn, rickety and leaning in the night mist, like some ghostly ship on shrouded seas. Nearby was a bog cottage dead in the jaws of sleep, its blind windows winking at the dying moon over Wicklow. Distantly, the town was awaking in door-slams and cries: the faint wail of a baby drifted on the mist; cattle bellowed, cocks began to crow and a steeple clock mournfully chimed in the dawn.

Aching from the fight with the Irish patriot, fevered with the pain of my injured hand, I led Mia to the barn and tethered her. Climbing on to a cart I leaped on to the hay, pulling myself up. Weariness overtook me in waves of increasing intensity: the ride from Wexford was taking its toll: exhausted, I slept. In a feather-bed of hay; in the sweet, earth-smell of the farm I slept, and did not dream.

I awoke just before midday, and lay in the drowsy stupor of comfort; and yet with my eyes still closed, I knew that I was not alone. I sensed the danger, but could not recognize it. This is the smell of death that comes to the pegged savage before the raking horn and the scream: this is the scent of the lynx, the foulness of the festering claws of the tiger before the leap. Instinctively, I shifted my injured hand towards the rapier at my side, and gripped the hilt.

'Ach, no you don't,' said a voice. 'You'll lie still, me son, or I'll have you on the end of this pitchfork.'

I opened my eyes. Standing above me was a little gnome of a man with a beard to his chest and a head as bald as pink ivory: rather like a leprechaun he looked standing there, feet astride me, but the pitchfork in his bunched little fists was rock steady. I sat up, watching him.

'Will ye tell me what you're up to in me barn, with not so much as by me leave?'

'Sleeping,' I said, stupidly.

'Aye, I can see that. Had ye been on a barn dance I'd have heard ye. D'you realize you're takin' possession without offering rent for it? Sure to God, if I give any passing vagrant free bedding I'd be scratching a beggar's trews with holes in.'

'I am not a vagrant.'

'I can see that. Your mare alone is worth a king's ransom, and there's jewels in the hilt of that rapier if ye'll kindly take your hand from it.'

I did not trust him. The points of the pitchfork were needle-bright, and trembling. 'Who are ye?' he asked.

'A messenger.'

'Bless me soul,' said he, lowering the pitchfork. 'I've had some queer customers hoofing it in an' out of me hay-barn – I've had loyalists and patriots, debtors and bailiffs; I've had runaway servants and drunken gentry sleepin' it off. But I've never had a King's messenger.' He eyed me. 'I did not say I was a King's messenger,' I replied softly.

'I'm glad ye didn't,' he replied merrily. 'For there's

gold in the pocket of a man who carries for the King, and he'd be carousing in the best inn of Wicklow, not skulking here in Patrick O'Toole's barn at twopence a night, for this is what it'll cost ye.' He put out his hand and I gave him twopence.

But he still stood on guard and I knew I would have to give an explanation. If he was a loyalist he would have the yeomanry on my heels the moment I left him: if he was a patriot he would let me hide till nightfall. This is the moment when the risk is taken, but it must be calculated. I said:

'Do you love Ireland, Mr O'Toole?'

'Like me soul.'

I rose, brushing myself down, and he followed me down to the cart where Mia opened one large brown eye at me and closed it again in sleep.

'Are you a patriot?' I asked.

At this he scratched his head, nonplussed and raised his puzzled little face to mine. 'It's a difficult question. If the rebellion comes and I call meself a King's man, me own flesh and blood will burn that cabin and fire this barn. And if the British dragoons come and I'm wearing the green, they'll tie me to a tree and hand me five hundred lashes in case I'm hiding arms. Can ye tell me what a fella best do?'

This was the tragedy of Ireland. It was the little men, like these, who suffered most on the eve of the Rebellion. They couldn't tell friend from foe: as traitors to the cause they could be shot by the patriots or suffer half-hanging and flogging by Irishmen loyal to the

British crown, or even the terror of the blazing cap, the indescribable torture of the Hessians.

There are times, as my father once said, when I weep for my country.

'Will you let me stay till nightfall, Mr O'Toole?' I asked.

'And why should I?' His beard trembled with indignation. 'Sure, it's fine for you if it's true you're a patriot messenger, but how do I stand if the North Cork Militia come?'

'That is the chance you take.'

'Is that right? Well, I'm not takin' it, so you can hoof your way out of here as soon as ye like.'

'It is important that I stay, Mr O'Toole.'

'And it's important to me that ye go.'

I said, evenly, 'You can't sit on the fence, man. You're either for or against the Rebellion, so you've got to make up your mind.'

'But the thing isn't even started yet!' He glared at me.

'Give it a week,' I said.

He crossed himself, head bowed. 'Then God help us. God help all in this forsaken country.'

'She is not forsaken. She is not forsaken by God or the patriots, though she may be by the likes of you. It's no good loving the beloved land if you're not prepared to die for it.'

He said, huskily, his face averted: 'It's the courage I lack, young 'un.'

'Aye, most of the time I'm scared to death – we all lack courage, Mr O'Toole.'

He grunted. 'Aye, but some more than others.' Moodily, he turned away, and I pitied him. Leaning on the cart, he said, 'See that farm over there? It was a two-acre patch, and run by young Mike Collins and his pretty wife. Two years back they married and started raisin' potatoes and children, and the place looked fine, though it was mainly scrub-land when he got it off the landlord.'

'What happened?' I asked, for tears were in his eyes when he turned to me.

He replied, 'Well, young Mike had a friend – the Wicklow blacksmith. Five days a week the blacksmith shoed, but on the sixth day he forged pikeheads on his anvil, and young Mike, he whittled and fashioned the handles and buried them in boxes on his patch.'

I knew what was coming, and turned away. I heard him say:

'And a week last Monday the Militia came, and then the Redcoats. Somebody had informed. They dug and found the pikes, they hanged the blacksmith in his forge; they hanged young Mike Collins before his own front door.'

With an effort, I said, 'It is the price we pay for being patriots, Patrick O'Toole.'

'O, aye?' He spat at my feet and wiped his mouth with the back of his hand. 'Do not talk to me about patriotism, for I am too long in the tooth. I've only a few years left in me, but I don't intend to lose them on a lost cause. They've got the country by the throat, an' you know it, for all your fine talk. You and the likes of Mike Collins can die if ye like, but me, Patrick O'Toole,

I'm stayin' alive.' He flung down the pitchfork and walked out of the barn, a strangely squat little figure with his hairless head, long white beard and wrinkled trews and peasant doublet. Turning, he called, 'So you clear out o' here as soon as ye like or I'm ridin' me donkey hell for leather for the yeomanry of Wicklow, and then, God rest ye soul.'

It was dangerous to travel by day. Normally, it was a risk that I was never prepared to take, especially now, for the closer I got to Dublin the thicker were the British patrols. For although Joe Lehane said the roads were clear between Castlekevin and Bray, apart from wandering troops of Redcoats, it was known that road-blocks and dragoon regiments were abounding south of Dublin city.

Now I looked at the sky. It was cobalt blue fleeced with billowing, washday clouds of St Peter's Friday, and the sun burned down with incinerating heat. On a morning such as this the flash of a bridle or the scabbard of a rapier – even a pistol-butt, could be seen for a mile.

'Get going,' commanded O'Toole, 'or as God's me judge I'll sell you in Wicklow.'

'I wouldn't be the first, would I?'

It halted him in his tracks and he turned back to me: agony was in his face and his body began to tremble. I said, 'You talk half-truths, man – you never talk straight.'

He clenched his hands, shrieking, 'You get going, ye dirty rebel, or I'll not be responsible!'

'You sold Mike Collins,' I said evenly. 'I can see it in your face.'

'I did not! I swear I did not!'

'You informed on your friend, man. You're the dregs of manhood, you're the gutter of Ireland.'

'Get out!'

I replied, saddling Mia, 'Aye, I will, for I'd not be seen dead in your company. And if I'd known the dirt you are I'd have shared a bed with the rats of Wicklow and taken my chance with the Military than bedding down here under your roof.'

He did not reply, and when I turned he was on his knees, knuckling his face with his fists and whimpering. Strangely, I pitied him: these are the weaklings of life: these are the cringers who beg and plead, while others know the strength of manhood and a life well lived: such as these can spit in the faces of their tormentors and place their lives in the hands of their God.

Yet I heard myself say, pitilessly, 'Right, I'm away. Now hasten down to Wicklow and inform on me.'

'Forgive me, forgive me,' he mumbled in his prayer, weeping tunelessly.

'Do not ask it of me,' I said, 'Ask it of your God.'

Mounting Mia, I reined her to the barn entrance, and instantly drew her back into the shelter of the hay.

A redcoat dragoon troop of some hundred men were riding down the road from Wicklow, and heading for the farm. Booted and spurred they came, their red coats flashing in the brilliant sunlight, their sabres clanking, their lances and pennants streaming in the wind.

Trapped, I backed Mia deep into the hay, put my hands over her muzzle and whispered in her ear, begging her to silence.

'Your country has given you another chance, man,' I said to Patrick O'Toole.

8 Traitor or patriot?

FINE and handsome they looked, these English dragoons, the men of the southern counties, the *élite* of the British army who later sabred the French gunner at the battle of Waterloo and laughed at the cavalry of Napoleon as they charged across open plains. They trotted into the farmyard of Patrick O'Toole, and wheeled in formation, an officer leading, and O'Toole, hands clenched in his terror, walked unsteadily to meet them.

And then my own heart nearly stopped beating.

Behind the officer rode the sergeant who had questioned me in Joe Lehane's place at Enniscorthy: square and strong he sat his horse, his bright, blue eyes roving the stackyard, seeing everything at a glance. One glimpse, and he would recognize me; this I knew. And if he saw me now it would not only mean my own death, but that of Joe Lehane, and even Kathleen. I bowed my head: the bile rose in my throat at the thought of it. The officer, fair-faced and young, cried:

'Has a man on a big, black mare passed this way, Irishman?'

Through a fork in straw I could see O'Toole's face and terror was in him.

'Speak up, man,' bellowed the sergeant. 'No need to

be afraid. Have you seen a big fair lad on a black mare pass the place?'

'They're comin' and goin' night and day,' cried O'Toole, his voice as high as a woman's. 'Sure, they're as thick as fleas in Chinese bedding, an' I don't know one from the other.'

I closed my eyes with relief. And he was surprising me: courage is a strange, elusive quality, and rides safest on the back of humour.

'You're sure, now?' cried the officer.

'If we find a strange hoof on this patch,' shouted the sergeant, 'you'll get the rope before you account for it.'

'Ach, dear heaven!' cried O'Toole, becoming bolder, 'am I likely to be hiding an enemy of the people when I gave the name of Mike Collins himself, to say nothin' of the blacksmith?' He approached the officer. 'Don't ye remember me, your worship? I'm the fella who put ye on to the pikes, and though you promised me gold I've seen no sign of it.'

Disdain was on the officer's face. He took from his pocket a gold piece and dropped it in the mud at his horse's feet. And the sergeant idly said:

'There's a stink in the nostrils of decent men, sir, for I could never stomach an informer.' He tightened his rein. 'I think I'll look round the farm just the same since the others can buy dirt as easily as we can,' and he turned his horse's head towards the barn and trotted directly towards me.

Sometimes I see that scene now: the bright scarlet of the Redcoat troop, the officer in his cavalry blue, and Patrick O'Toole, the informer, grovelling at the feet of his horse for the gold that hanged Mike Collins, the patriot. But as the sergeant spurred his horse towards the barn, he rose and cried:

'Run for it, son, run for it in the name of Ireland!'

And while they were milling and prancing around the farmyard I was across Mia's back and down the road to Wicklow like a hare coursing, with pistol-balls whining overhead and swishing through the hedges. I looked back but once, I remember.

Patrick O'Toole, the informer, I saw among that milling redness of the soldiers' tunics: and he was laughing at the sky, hands on hips in the second before a sabre flashed from its scabbard, and cut him down.

I am older now, as I write this, my first youth gone. And I have met some men in my time, men who would die before denying their creed of living, or their God. But I have never since met a man like Patrick O'Toole, the informer, who lost his soul when they hanged his friend on a Monday, and found it again eleven days later on that St Peter's Friday.

They did not catch me, of course: for all their talk of English bloodstock, you've got to come to Ireland for real horse-breeding. Mia was as fresh and cheeky as a daisy after her sleep, and we didn't see the going of them.

And as we streaked across the bright, green country west of the spires of Wicklow, I breathed a prayer for the soul of an informer.

The road was clear of patrols between Castlekevin and Bray, just as Joe Lehane said it would be. But for safety's sake I took Mia down to the strand when Bray came up on the skyline, for the tide was thundering in, and this would destroy our hoof-prints. And as we galloped along in a mist of spray, I saw above the white-foamed breakers a warship at anchor off Bray, her Union Jack a splash of blood in the fierce sunlight, for the sun was setting over the rim of the world as big as a Dutch cheese with him, hissing in sea-mist. Reining in, I took Mia to the entrance of a cave, and here we rested, waiting for the veil of night. For perhaps an hour I sat there watching the sea, and saw a long-boat leave the English frigate and move in a black dot over the rocky promontory west of Bray. Nearby Mia was grazing happily, munching of the succulent vetch-grass of the dunes, the hair of the beach.

'All right for you,' I said, and she raised her head and rolled an eye at me, snorting reply.

'You can find a dinner anywhere,' I said, and at this she turned her back upon me.

There was a great hunger in me, and I laid back, cradling my head in my hands, listening to sea-thunder and dreaming of Joe Lehane's and a great round of beef surloin sizzling and spluttering on the spit, with his little spit-dog Nell turning it on the wheel. I must have slept a bit, for I recall I dreamed of thick red slices of it clamped between door-step bread, and an ale pewter to wash it down, and Kathleen coming up with great wedges of cold rice-pudding, and are you sure you've had enough, John Regan, because there's more for the asking, and welcome.

Bats and darkness were dropping over the land when

I awoke with my stomach lying on my backbone. The sea was emblazoned with a silver moon now, the evening star making the sign of the cross in her sky of God. Suddenly, there was a strange nearness in me for my mother. Pale and proud was my mother in the portrait my father kept in his study back home in Milford; beautiful, she looked, she who gave her life for me.

So with Mia standing over me, waiting to be gone, I knelt in the sand and prayed for my mother whose name was Mary.

When the prayer was over Mia came up behind me and pushed me over with her muzzle, being ready to move, she being a great one for a change of scenery.

'Right, you,' I said, 'but now it's my turn to be eating.'

The bulge of the letter was a comfort under my fingers as I mounted Mia and took up the beach and along the moonlit road to Bray.

Light and smoke struck me in the face as I opened the door of the Black Boar Tavern. A score of faces turned to view the stranger.

A mixed bag, by the look of it: gentry faces of arrogant stares; the teak-tanned faces of the agent-farmers, the sallow, work-lined faces of the cabin peasants. And the bright eyes of a serving-maid sparkled at me, since she, too, was young. I entered the low-beamed room in a pin-drop silence. And the landlord recovered first as I reached his counter, his gaunt, cavernous face peering at me from the coffin of his soul.

' 'Evenin', zur.'

' 'Evening,' I replied.

The oppression of the room beat about me. For this was Ireland on the eve of revolution, and the nearer you got to Dublin the stronger the smell of gunpowder: few men trusted their friends these days, let alone strangers. Turning my back on the room, I slapped down silver.

'A tankard of that home-brew, landlord, and a round or two of beef for a man near starved to death.'

'Aye, zur.' He bent to a cask, filling a foaming pewter. 'Biddy, me girl – a plate of beef for the young gentleman, and hurry.'

'Comin'!'

The landlord pushed the pot towards me. 'Come far?'

'Enniscorthy.'

'You native there, son?'

I glanced over my shoulder. The speaker was aged, his paunchy face livid blue, with the drooping eyes of a hound, like a man struck by lightning.

'No, sir – just passing through.'

'Fine mare you got outside, I'm bound,' called another. This was a beefy farmer, and I judged him as a small landlord.

'Fine money I reckon he paid for it!' laughed his companion.

The room warmed to me. A room becomes warm, I find, if you enter it with humility.

I said, 'My father's mare, and money couldn't buy her.'

'The Military will take no account of that, young 'un!' cried the landlord.

'The Military?'

A man shouted from a corner, 'British dragoons are

taking all horses within five miles of Dublin – paying a golden guinea, and sabres coming out if ye so much as question it!'

'Where you bound?' whispered the peasant close to me.

'Dublin,' I said, 'dragoons or not.'

'More luck to ye, son, I like ye guts, but ye won't get that mare within sight of the city of Dublin, so be warned.'

I sipped at the ale, for drink, it should be remembered, is linked to the tongue by taste and the stomach by sense. On a full stomach it can prove a friend; on an empty one ale can get you hanged, said my father.

The warmth and companionship of the room enveloped me. Though it was summer, a peat fire glowed in the open hearth, and around it, like men whose bones are cold with hunger, huddled the bog peasants, their eyes fevered in their pallid cheeks. They ate, but did not drink, and huddled closer to make room as I sat between them.

'Sit by here, man.'

This seat was convenient also, because I could command the door and see the comforting shadow of Mia on the bow window-glass. And then I saw a big man sitting in the shadows of a skew corner by the tap-bar. I sensed rather than saw his dark eyes examining me. And then, instantly, I recognized him as the man who had stayed the night at Joe Lehane's inn at Enniscorthy. He sat aside that skew seat exactly as he sat his horse on the morning he had left the stable yard.

I ate slowly, fighting down the desire to bolt the food,

for I was nearly faint with hunger, and the muffled conversation of the room beat about me: talk of the North Cork Militia mainly, and the patrols of British dragoons. And when I glanced up from my plate again I saw the eyes of the man in the corner full upon me, examining me with detailed interest, and I cursed my foolishness. It was my mention of Enniscorthy that had drawn his attention to me in the first place. His eyes above his glass were steady and calm; his hand was on the hilt of the rapier at his belt, and there was a strange hatred in his eyes as he lowered the glass.

Enniscorthy! The blood flew to my face in self-anger: these are the stupid mistakes that get a man hanged: this is the sort of stupidity that makes one unworthy of so sacred a trust.

'Another whiskey, Mister Barrington?' asked the landlord.

The big man rose. 'Thank you, no – I'd best be getting along.'

I remembered the Irish patriot who had attacked me outside Carnew, and flexed my swollen hand. Was this the Jonah Barrington of whom he had spoken? Was this the man he had tracked from Bargy Castle, the home of the patriot he called Bagenal Harvey, and Keugh, his friend? Was this the loyalist the patriot had mistaken me for – was this, indeed, the Jonah Barrington who was riding to Dublin to betray his friends with whom he had dined?

A yokel shouted, 'Reckon you'll get your horse safe to Dublin, sir, dragoons or not, eh, Mister Barrington?'

The man moved to the door. 'It's the horses of the

rebels they're mainly after, man, not decent law-abiding people.'

'O, ah?' said a peasant beside me, 'law abiding, is it? Old Ned Tamber had his cabin fired by the North Cork night 'fore last, an' he was law abidin' enough for any man.'

'Old Ned's likely to lose his neck before he's finished, mind!' cried another, and the landlord said bitterly, making a fist of his hand:

'The country's going stark ravin' mad, Mister Barrington. You're a big man in Wexford, what with dining with the squires, and such-like. So you speak for the likes of us when you get to Dublin, for it's a scandal.'

Jonah Barrington replied evenly, 'Speak for you, I will, if you show respect for law and order.'

'Law and order, is it, zur?' shouted the peasant beside me. 'Night 'fore last, they come, just like Simon said – an' they burned Ned Tamber's cabin an' sent him and his missus down the road to the poorhouse, and the pair of 'em God-fearin' people, remember.'

'He must have done something wrong,' replied Mr Barrington.

'Aye, be fair to the gentlemun, Sam – old Ned's got a son who's a United Irishman, remember that, too.'

'If he had a son who is a rebel to the Irish nation, he deserves to lose his cabin!'

'Nothin' to do with old Ned what his son is up to, mind!'

Their voices rose in anger and dissent, and slowly the room split down the middle: on one hand people claiming the need for law and order: on the other hand men claiming the needs for justice and shouting their hatred of those oppressing them. And I saw that night, in that room, the tragedy of my country: I saw the divided factions, of rich against poor; or loyalist against rebel.

'Time the people took a hand!'

'Don't talk daft, man, what with one and the other of 'em they'd burn us, never mind our cabins!'

'Father O'Keefe himself did say it's a crying scandal, an' he's up this morning to see the Military about it. A good man is Ned Tamber.'

'Father wants to watch – they'll burn his church, never mind Ned's cabin.'

'Now then, now then, gentlemen...!' bawled the landlord.

They quarrelled, they shouted, they rose to their feet, their faces aflame with passion, and I pitied them.

The man Jonah Barrington said, 'Listen!'

Commanded by him, they were silenced: it was so quiet that I heard the wind sighing in the eaves and the distant thunder of the breakers. He said softly, 'From Antrim to Wexford, even in Dublin, there is talk of revolution. In Enniscorthy itself they are making arms. But let me tell you this – if this country goes into rebellion now, it will be the end of Ireland for the next century. For you've got the flag of Britain whether you like it or not, and you'll send it back to England by persuasion, not by force.'

'It's Ireland no more, man, and you know it,' whispered one.

'It's Ireland for everlasting,' said Barrington, 'and there's no truer heart in an Irish breast than mine. Do you want the land to run with blood? Do you want your cabins burned and your children sent to transportation? For if that's what you want you can have it for the asking, because you haven't got a chance. The land is swarming with British troops . . .'

'And they'd run helter-skelter at the first landing of the French!'

A babble of argument broke out then, and the landlord cried, 'Give Mister Barrington a hearing, men, for he's educated—hush quiet, now!'

Barrington cried, 'Didn't the French promise a landing before? Didn't fifteen thousand Frenchies come with a fleet under General Hoche and Wolfe Tone, but did they set foot in Bantry? And that was two years back.'

'The weather was against 'em, man, talk sense!' cried a peasant.'

'Wolfe Tone, Wolfe Tone!' They rose to their feet, calling the beloved name, but I did not move. Yet my blood thrilled to the sound of it. For although I had never met this famous Irish patriot who was enlisting the might of Bonaparte to free his country from the British yoke, I had heard his name constantly on my father's lips. A peasant, gaunt and rangy, leaped to his feet and cried, 'Sure, if Wolfe comes again it'll be a different tune he'll play. In '96 the god of the storms was against him, but he'll come again and save the country, an' we'll have a decent Irish Parliament instead of the one we're loaded with now!'

Roars and checrs at this.

'And do you know what that will mean, man?' asked

Barrington. 'It'll mean we'll have a French army of occupation instead of a British one; it's the devil you know and the devil you don't – and I, for one, would rather have the British, what say you, lad?'

He fixed his eyes on me, but I did not reply.

'Have ye no tongue, lad?' cried the landlord. 'Straighten it out and say your piece, for we are needing youngsters like you to make the future of the beloved country.'

I munched on steadily, refusing to be drawn. I dared not. One word out of place, one hint of my views, which were hot and feverish, might bring them about me and spell disaster for my mission.

'A still tongue keeps a wise head,' I answered in the silence.

'And if you back the law and the authority of the Parliament, you'll likely keep your head on your shoulders,' said Barrington, his hand on the door. 'The lad's given good counsel, and I ask the rest of you to remember it.'

Like a fool I sat there and watched him go, wondering if what the Irish patriot had told me was the truth.

9 Press-ganged!

AND I have often wondered since if he set the trap for me, for no man left that tap-room except Barrington.

I was on my feet, I remember, and on my way to the door when a peasant said:

'Sure, in truth ye look the part, me son, with your square jaw and wide shoulders, an' I'll swear you're six foot up, but I'll tell ye this.' And he rose beside me, his starved face turned up to mine. 'It's not the size of the man but the size of the fight in the man, an' from where I stand you look two foot-three.'

Another, a little wizened gnome of a man, tore off his coat and turned his lacerated back to me. 'Two hundred and fifty lashes they handed me, to tell them where the pikes were hidden.'

'But he didn't tell them,' said his friend, lifting his pewter.

'And this on me,' cried another, and tore off his broad-rimmed hat, and I bowed my head at the sight of him, for his scalp was burned hairless and stark white, and I knew he had suffered the terrible torture of the dreaded German Hessians – the blazing cap of pitch.

'An' he didn't tell where the powder was hidden, either,' said a fourth. His voice rose and he shouted into my face, 'So you can away to Dublin city itself and tell ye fine friends that the men of Kildare spit in their faces, for we'll rise with the rest of them in Wexford when the leaders tell us to rise, and no thanks to the likes of you who keeps a wise tongue.'

In such company of courage I could not lift my eyes to them.

'Goodbye,' I said.

'Good riddance!' They turned away in disgust of me. 'It's Ireland for ever for us, and the devil himself take those who sit on the fence.'

And as I went out of the door the press-gang came in, driving me backwards.

Six of them.

And brawny Jack Tar Englishmen, all six, with flat hats and pigtails tied and tarred, their broad chests rippling muscles under their tight black jerseys. Grinning, they came, closing the door behind them.

'There's a likely sample, Bos'n!' shouted one.

I drew the rapier, kicked away a table for room, and backed away to a wall. And the Irishmen laughed. Not one of them there was of serving-age for the British Navy, and they laughed like drunken leprechauns, stamping about the floor at my discomfiture, and while they laughed I inwardly cursed my own stupidity. I had seen the ship lying off Bray headland. All my life I had known that a single vessel working alone was a press-gang ship, for enough of them had entered Milford. And I had seen them at work in the Milford streets when the taverns turned out, for this was how the British Navy got its sailors – more than forty per cent of them through the press-gang system, when a man could be snatched from his own front door by force, to serve five years aboard Nelson's Navy, and his wife and children left to starve. I stiffened the rapier.

'Put that thing down,' whispered the Bos'n, 'or it'll be the worse for ye, son. Come peaceful in the King's name an' no harm'll befall ye.'

He winked and guffawed, and the sailors behind him roared approval.

'Just come quiet, lad, and rock in the cradle of the deep.'

'Sure to heaven!' cried an Irishman, 'ye can take him with pleasure, for he b'ant no good to us!'

I think I knew immediately that I had no chance, for two men at the rear drew their cutlasses and came to the front. The Bos'n said:

'Do you come in one piece, me hearty, or do we make it several?'

It was useless to fight with weapons, for I was of a seaport and knew the way of the Navy. If I killed one of them I would be arraigned before a naval court-martial on the frigate by morning and hang from its yard-arm at dusk, as an example to those who fought the press-gangs. I dropped the rapier.

'That's better,' grunted the Bos'n, and rushed.

I caught the leading man with a hard one to the jaw, but his onward rush sent me backwards, and immediately the others were upon me with fierce cries, tripping me and pinning me down. Somehow, I managed to squirm away and rose, hitting out, but they brought me to my knees and somebody struck from behind. As the lights of the room faded, I heard the landlord say:

'Give him credit. For all his talk of keeping a wise tongue, he behaves for all the world like a man.'

I awoke in darkness to the creaking of oars and the rolling slap of water, and opened my eyes. The stars, I remember, were so big in the black velvet sky that it seemed I could have reached up and touched them. I did not move. Through half-closed eyes I took in my surroundings, and was at once aware that my hands and legs were tied; and brutally tied, so that the cord bit deep into the flesh of my wrists and ankles. Before me sat a brawny English tar straining at an oar, his head and shoulders moving over the stars in the rhythm of his labour: other men were behind him, also rowing. Behind me the unmistakable voice of the Bos'n shouted:

'Keep at it, me lads. We got a thin haul tonight, an' the Captain won't thank us for missing the tide.'

'These Irish weigh heavy, mind!' cried a man. 'Solid in the shoulders and lead between the ears, they say.'

'Bos'n!' bawled another from the prow of the boat, 'do you realize that young fella hit me with a fist for knocking in nails? An' I've a lump on me chin like a duck's egg, and sparking.'

'Next time you'll learn to ride it, Sam!'

'And me Kildare Irish, too – press-ganging me own flesh and blood, it is. Sure, ye have to kill a hundred Irishmen to get a pound of brains.'

They shouted with laughter. In the British Navy at about this time there were more pure Irishmen than any other nationality: and the dogged tars who fought under Nelson at the Battle of Trafalgar a few years later and fought with him at the Battle of the Nile were men of every Irish county.

As the long-boat lumbered on I became aware that I was not the only prisoner. No less than three men were lying about me in the stern around the splayed legs of the Bos'n at the tiller, and I could see the boots of another two up for'ard.

'Are ye comfortable, me lucky lads?' shouted the Bos'n. 'You're in good company, ye see, for I'm as Irish as the shamrock, and I'm partial to ye, like Sam up in front.'

'Will you loose these ropes, then?' asked a prisoner.

'If I do that ye'll be up and swinging again, and I'm after getting you before Captain Simmons in one piece, so be patient.'

A man lying beside me cried. 'You loosen these ropes, Bos'n, and I'll raise cuts on your cursed Irish crew that you'll carry to your grave!'

'Ach, dear me, hark at it! He's after beatin' us black and blue, and us just poor Irish Jack tars doin' our duty by the King of England – there's gratitude for ye, an' you an Englishman. Don't ye want to see the world, son?'

'I'll see you dead first!' It was the voice of a young man, and cultured.

The crew bawled laughter, and the Bos'n cried with glee, 'Now, me boy, ye mustn't strain yourself or the Captain'll get his paddy up an' ye'll get a rope's end or a keel-hauling to cool you, and that'd be a tremendous pity.'

'He can do his worst,' came the defiant reply, 'but he won't break me.'

'That, me son, remains to be seen,' said the Bos'n. 'Haul away, me lovely boyos, haul away for the love of England, for she's the queen o' the seas!'

And to my amazement, the crew took this up, chanting to the rhythmic heaving of the oars:

'We heat our cannon at the Frenchies,
We ravage the coast of Spain,
We scrub and haul and quarrel and brawl
From Dover to the Main
For the gold of another man's gain, me boys,
For the land of another man's birth,
But though he's king of the seas, boys,
Ould Ireland's the flower of the earth.'

The boat sped on. I clenched my eyes and turned away my face, thankful for the darkness. For these were pure-bred Irishmen who were capturing their brothers for forced service to a foreign king. And in their ignorance, in their blind acceptance of a foreign domination they were selling their birthright while still retaining their dogged love for their country.

10 The *Sea-Hawk*

As we slid alongside the black hulk of the brig, a bearded face peered down from the gunwale. A brig she was, though I had taken her for a frigate.

'Ahoy, there, Bos'n, are your nets full, man?'

Bull-chested and tall, the Bos'n rose up. 'Ach, 'tis only six, but none of them sprats. It's five husky Irish an' an Englishman who's goin' to belt the livin' daylights out o' us!'

'Then haul him up first, Bos'n, an' we'll start the belting!'

Gusts of raucous laughter at this, and cheers, with jerseyed British tars lining the poop rail and shouting down insults, and I looked towards the shore of Bray where the yellow lights were dimming in a gathering mist, and thought of Mia tethered outside the Black Boar Tavern – there for anybody's taking: there for any passing tramp, including the precious letter in her saddle for Lord Edward Fitzgerald.

I clenched my hands and cursed myself for stopping for food.

Now, instead of fulfilling the mission my father had died for, I would be hundreds of miles out at sea by the end of the week. The young Englishman beside me stirred in his bonds, and whispered:

'Are you English, man?'

'Irish,' I replied.

He groaned. 'Heaven help us, me especially. I was in a coach with my wife and baby, making for Lucan to start a new life. And they reined us in and hauled us out – the one on the other side of you is the driver.'

'Rest yourself,' I said. 'There's a dozen decent men passing on the coach roads, and any of them will take a woman and baby to Lucan.'

'I pray to God for them.'

'Pray for yourself,' I answered, 'for you've a temper on you like a wild ass, and you'll end on the main-mast for a flogging.'

He turned to me in the dim light of the boat's lantern, and his face was one as if chiselled from granite, with a fine square jaw on him and his eyes spoiling for a fight. He said through his teeth: 'Don't you set a price on liberty? Don't you writhe inside at being shipped aboard this stinking hulk like cattle?'

'I'm saving my strength for other things, and so should you.'

'Not me. The moment I'm free I'm taking that Bos'n.'

'You're too handy with your tongue, man, and you should keep your hands to yourself. Don't you want to get to Lucan with your family?'

'Aye, with all my heart.'

'Then pocket your fists and save them for the get-away. Can ye swim?'

'No.'

'It's an excellent start,' I said.

Now we bumped the *Sea-Hawk*'s side, and the name

on her stern blazed down at me. Derricks were swung out; our boat crew hitched up, and we slowly rose up the brig's tarred hull. From her gun embrasures and tiny cabin holes there came the stink of decaying food and unwashed bodies, and the smell of her was one worse than a pig-sty, then some. This was the manner in which England commanded the seas: by keeping her sailors in the floating hovels that the admirals called the pride of England. With the lash in constant use and keel-hauling rampant, this was how she dominated the navies of the world. And the astonishing fact was that she received, in return, the undying valour and patriotism of her crews. True, there had been mutinies, like the last big one off Spithead, but rebellions against the terrible conditions aboard were few. A yard-arm hanging was the last embrace of the Admiralty, it was said, and sailors were flogged and hanged in hundreds.

The long-boat reached the deck of the brig, and I raised myself at the Bos'n's feet, staring along the dripping decks. I judged her at about 170 tons; seeing her guns staring through their breechings already restrained for action – one long six-pounder at the prow and stern; six ten-pounders ranged lar and starboard. And while eager hands reached into the long-boat and hauled out the prisoners, I saw above me her great twin masts and square-rigged sails already billowing, and she was straining at the anchor like a chained leopard, heeling and pitching to the big sea coming up. They cut our bonds. Surrounded by tars with drawn cutlasses, we were lined up against a bulkhead.

'Captain's comin'!' said the Bos'n.

Glowering, we stood in line, all six of us, the Englishman beside me, and I saw immediately that, although I topped him by at least three inches, he was built like a prize-fighter and raring to go. I muttered:

'Keep that temper under your shirt, man, or they'll flog all six of us.'

The captain approached, walking carelessly through the bedlam of labour, for sailors were appearing from everywhere now. From the prow came their chanting song as they wheeled the capstan, and the little ship heeled violently as she came free into the wind.

'A motley lot, Bos'n,' observed the captain, a little bespectacled man more like an office clerk than captain of this vicious little fighting ship.

'Had to take 'em as they came, Captain, sir, begging ye pardon, sir,' said the Bos'n.

'They don't get any better, do they?'

'That they don't, sir. Reckon we've had the best of 'em, mind. Though there's fighters among 'em, like this one.' And he jerked his thumb at me. 'Raised lumps on poor old Sam O'Shea, and threatened me wi' a rapier, he did.'

'Excellent.' The captain paused before me, his little grey eyes boring into mine. The ship suddenly heeled to the wind, then, and sailors slipped and fell, cursing, but the man watching me didn't even move: a man born of the sea.

'A rapier, eh? That's unusual. What is your name?'

'Shaun Casey, sir,' I lied.

'And where are you from?' His voice was bass and strangely beautiful.

'Milford.'

'Kindly address me as "sir" every time you speak to me, or I will consider you impertinent, d'you understand?'

'Yes, sir.'

'You sound educated. Are you?'

I did not reply, for he suddenly shouted, 'Mr Soper, where the devil are you?'

'Here, sir, coming, sir!' A flushed mate appeared.

'The glass is dropping, is it not?'

'Aye, sir.'

'Then shorten sail – get another reef in the tops'ls. Quartermaster, can you hear me?' He bellowed astern.

'Aye aye, sir!' came the faint wail aft.

'N'east by east, and make it lively!' The captain glanced at the sky. Thunder-clouds were gathering in the caverns of the heavens, barging and shouldering their way across the world as if in haste to deluge it with water.

The deck shivered beneath us as the *Sea-Hawk* answered the helm, and she heeled to larboard, sensing a tack. The wind howled in the rigging, the sails floundered and bellied like things demented, and the captain was unperturbed. His eyes did not leave mine when he said:

'A rapier, eh? Where were you bound, young man?'

'Dublin city, sir.'

'On what errand?'

'To visit me aunt, sir.'

'Indeed. And from where do you hail, did you say?'

'Milford, sir.'

The *Sea-Hawk* pitched and rolled like a live thing. The captain said:

'It is a long cry from Milford to Dublin. Were you horsed?'

'Yes, sir.'

'And you insist that your name is Shaun Casey? I fancy that it flew too readily to your tongue. If you are lying to me I will have you flogged, do you understand that?'

'Yes, sir.'

He turned away from me. 'Watch this one, Bos'n. He answers too politely for innocence, for he is boiling inside. But there'll be time enough to get the truth of him.'

'Aye, sir – time enough!'

'Get all six of them on the capstan, and give them the rope's end if they slacken.'

'Break them early, sir, that's the motto!'

'By heaven,' muttered the Englishman beside me, 'if he takes a rope's end to me I'll not be responsible. . . !'

'D'you want to see your wife and kid again, man?'

He stared at me, and I said, 'If you do, you'll behave now. There's all the time in the world to lay one on his whiskers later.'

'Come on, come on!' commanded the Bos'n, 'look lively!'

'Aye aye, sir,' I said.

And as we bent to the capstan to heighten the anchor, the *Sea-Hawk* heaved over as if trying to escape the mad rush of the sea, for the wind was rising and howling in the rigging. Above me, swinging against the stars, I saw the sailors clinging to the cordage, and the harsh commands of the Bos'n rose above the wind:

'Get the top foresails in, men. Set the mainmast stays fair!'

The captain emerged from a companionway. 'Mr Soper! It's going to be a dirty night, and the glass is lower...' The mainsail volleyed and thundered.

'Glass right down, Captain!'

'So heave to, and we'll wait for morning.'

'You realize the French'll be off Dublin by morning, sir?'

'I have not forgotten, Mr Soper.'

'Two frigates, sir, remember?'

'I am aware of it, Mr Soper. You heave to, and leave the French to me.'

'Aye aye, sir!' The mate roared, 'Get those foretops in, lads.' He swung to aft, lifting his speaking-horn. 'Quartermaster, bring her to!'

'Bring her to, sir!' came the faint reply.

Now we swam with the wind: the larboard main-shrouds took the wind and we lazed on the breast of the sea instead of fighting for quarter.

And, despite my predicament, there grew within me a strange and strong emotion: it was as if a new and wild sense of freedom was snatching me up, making me one with the elements.

With the deck slippery beneath my feet, I strained against the capstan arm to the metallic clattering of the anchor chain. The Englishman behind me said:

'By morning we'll be fifty miles from Bray, Irishman, you realize it?'

I did not reply.

This, I thought, might easily depend upon the French.

Despite the captain's confident reply, I knew – and he knew – that if he met two frigates they would blast him out of the sea.

And the heavens opened in a vicious fork of lightning that lit the canopy of the sky. Thunder crashed and rolled, crashed again and reverberated in bass boomings across the oceans to the rim of the world.

The little captain glanced at the sky.

'It appears we are in for a dirty night, Mr Soper,' said he.

'It be gettin' a lot worse till it comes a lot better, beggin' ye pardon, sir,' remarked the Bos'n.

Despite myself I had to grin. I knew now why they ruled the sea.

11 Sea battle

OUT of an avalanche of darkness came the dawn in a cut-throat sky of blood, and I staggered out of the evil-smelling bunk into a world flat calm and hazed. All night we had tossed and rolled in green troughs, while all about me the press-gang prisoners had retched and vomited to the bellowing amusement of the hardened sailors. A summer wind stroked my face as I walked the slippery decks, and, to my astonishment, I could see the shore clearly, and the unmistakable outline of Bray. The *Sea-Hawk* was becalmed: the sails hung like dish-rags from her tops and main booms; the zephyr wind scarcely moved the flag at her stern.

High in the crow's-nest came the familiar wail, and I listened, my breathing pent, for his words were unintelligible. But others heard it, and the whole ship's company was galvanized into activity. Up the companionways flooded the sailors; instantly the world had become alive. And then I heard the cry again:

'Sail on the lee bow, sir!'

In the stuttering panic of the deck the Bos'n came, pulling men aside, and the mate leaped at the main-shrouds and hoisted himself up, telescope level.

'A frigate, sir!' he shouted down as the captain came up, buttoning his tunic. 'Looks French by the rake of her. Nay, sir – wait – two ships, but the other might be a brig.'

'Is she under sail, Mr Soper?'

'The frigate sails full, by the look of her – the brig seems becalmed.'

The captain idly turned, calling, 'Master-at-arms stand by. Mr Soper, run out the guns!'

'Aye aye, sir!'

The Englishman ran beside me then, whispering, 'What is happening?' Gaunt and pale he looked after a night of sea-sickness.

'A frigate and a brig coming up starboard,' I replied.

'French?'

'So the mate says – listen, this might be our chance.'

The captain cried, 'Arm the crew, Mr Soper – all except the new intakes.' He smiled thinly, approaching us. 'You are lucky men. Less than ten hours aboard a King's ship and you are about to see action. I was three years before I took my first broadside off Cadiz.' He turned, crying, 'Have the men breakfasted, Bos'n?'

'Aye, sir, all bellies full.'

'Then we'll see how they fight – a round of grog, remember, for the first Frenchman down. Can you go about, Mr Soper?'

'Short of wind, sir!'

'Yet they are coming fast. That is strange.' The captain took the glass and scanned the horizon.

'The brig's stopped, sir, – frigate's got the headland wind, we'll get her first, Captain!'

'In more ways than one, Mr Soper. Hands to the

sheets, please. Stand to your guns, men. And stand you will, remember. For you'll have to take a few French broadsides before we come within range.'

I looked at this man. This was the product of an English education – public school and university, without a doubt, and with the countenance of a merchant-banker. He was the pillar of this ship; he was brutal, so the men said, for he would order a flogging for the slightest misdemeanour; and yet they worshipped him. And now he was driving them to battle with a French frigate and a brig in support: out-ranged and out-gunned. On the face of it this was suicide, yet none questioned him.

A little wind blew from the headland then and instantly the wheel went over again, bringing the Frenchman on the larboard tack: slowly, lumbering before the breeze, the *Sea-Hawk* began to move.

'Powder-monkeys, powder-monkeys forward!' yelled the Bos'n, and six little ragged boys came running along the deck to larboard.

'You ready, boys?'

'Aye, ready, Bos'n,' cried one, breathless; I judged him at no more than thirteen years old.

'Right, then, and the first one of ye I see backing under the rail gets the boot, understand? You fetch and carry, or by thunder ...' He swung to me. 'You and the Englishman help with the powder. Like as not you'll blow to Kingdom Come, but you'll blow in fine company. Here, Willie and Tom will show you, an' you're under their orders.'

'Aye aye, sir,' I said.

He pulled a pistol from his belt. 'And anyone with

ideas about slippin' over the side gets a hole in the head big enough to sink him.'

Unaccountably, I was filled with a growing excitement. One side of me was praying that the Frenchmen would sink us, the other side longed to see the enemy pounded into oblivion. And I think I knew at that very moment, what it was that kept the British sailor loyal to these ferocious masters, and faithful to the Crown.

'Come on, come on!' cried Willie the powder-monkey, and we followed him and little Tom, scrambling down steps to the ship's magazine. Here men were working stripped to the waist, rolling in the shot and canister, and men on the deck above were winching them topside. But the powder was individually carried, and this was the work of the powder-monkeys. Up on deck now, a canister in each hand, and the pair of us served the guns where the master-gunners were waiting by the cannon, their sights trained on the oncoming Frenchmen. The captain cried then:

'They are taking us either side, Mr Soper. And the brig is making a rare speed. We will eat her first, gunners. The *Sea-Hawk*, too, is entitled to breakfast!'

The men roared at this, bending to the guns.

'Luff a little – steady at that!'

'Steady at that, sir!'

'Give her canister, if you please, Mr Soper!'

'Canister it is, sir!'

'And a broadside to clear her decks as she takes to larboard – forget the frigate, the French are poor shots.'

I was just emerging from the companionway when the frigate fired off starboard. Puffs of white smoke appeared along her hull, then long-tongued, red flashes of flame spat viciously. In a growing, thundering scream the fourteen twenty-four pound balls roared overhead. It was an astonishing crescendo of sound, as if the world itself was erupting. Distantly, on the larboard side, huge water-spouts rose lazily against the horizon.

'Give her target-practice, Mr Soper,' cried the captain. 'We will have the brig first, if you care. On target, master-gunner?'

'Right on target, sir!'

The brig, a little smaller than the *Sea-Hawk,* was tacking beautifully, and fearlessly closing the gap between us, for the wind had risen and she was under full sail. The range closed: the brig was but three hundred yards distant now.

'She is coming well,' called the captain. 'Fire when you are ready, Mr Soper – I want her rigging, remember.'

I rushed down the gun-alley, slid a canister of powder at the feet of the crew and peered above the bulwark an instant before the crash.

'Fire!'

The concussion flung me back against the bulkhead, and the *Sea-Hawk* heeled over to the kick of the six ten-pounders: the morning blazed red light, the canister shot whined across the sea, instantly, it seemed, catching the French brig square. Great splinters of wood flew skyward; her rigging sagged and folded dangerously, then her mainmast collapsed, tearing down top-sails, mizzens and main boom. A great hurrah rose from the gun-deck of the *Sea-Hawk.*

'Well done, gunners,' called the captain. 'Quite good shooting. Please go about, Mr Soper; larboard gunners prepare; go about when you are ready.'

'Hard over!' yelled the mate, and the *Sea-Hawk* heeled to the rising wind and churned at the sea with a curve of foaming wake behind her, and her big cannon spouted fire simultaneously with the courageous French brig. The ship shuddered beneath me. From below came the shrieking of men as the starboard deck blew upwards behind the foremast, lifting a ten-pounder gun and its crew of four lazily up into the blue. The *Sea-Hawk* listed to the impact of the broadside that had caught her square.

'Down mains!' roared Mr Soper, and we shivered at the sea where smoke-water plumes were rising from the cannonades of the frigate. Closer, closer she came, the first broadside straddling us, the third aimed for the splintering kill. Again and again the *Sea-Hawk*'s larboard gunners crashed their broadsides into the brave little brig. Dismasted, out of control, she drifted aimlessly while the ten-pound balls tore and raked her, and her sails lay over her like death-shrouds, for she had given her life so the frigate could close on us. Then, suddenly, with a tremendous roar, she blew up in a white-blaze explosion and we seemed to lift bodily out of the sea momentarily: cannon, debris, masts, sails and timbers rose into the air with incredible slowness, and came crashing into the sea about us. Dense, acrid smoke billowed over the gap, a desperate shield from the oncoming frigate, and in the medley of shrieks and yells I heard the captain's voice, calm and clear:

'Lay alongside, Mr Soper, if you please. Boarders prepare. Master-at-arms, where the devil are you? Issue cutlasses, and pikes out – yes, the new men also. Quartermaster, bring her round.'

'Bring her round, sir!'

'And Mr Soper!'

'Aye aye, sir?'

'Take her with a starboard broadside as she comes in, she will not like that, I vow.'

'Master gunner, prepare starboard broadside!'

'Gunners ready, sir!'

Dimly, through the billowing smoke came the dull-toned boom of the frigate's big cannon and tongues of flame spouted through the mist, and almost immediately the *Sea-Hawk* replied. The big balls were rammed home, smashing into the Frenchman, smashing into the *Sea-Hawk*; ramming down through decks and cabins, leaving a bloody trail of ripped hammocks and crippled men, and I will remember their shrieks until the end of my days. And then, with these last crashing blows, the two ships collided, the frigate taking us at the bow. With rigging crashing down, they became entangled momentarily, then the sea leaped between us, forcing them apart. Again and again the *Sea-Hawk*'s carronades barked out, and the long-gun in the prow came roaring in with grape-shot, sweeping the tangled decks of the Frenchman. I was following young Willie up the companionway with a tin of powder in each hand, serving the guns of an English ship without realizing it: I was praying for an English victory at a time of my own, personal disaster. I could not help it. At that moment of ultimate conflict it was no longer England against Ireland or rebel against dragoon. It was Great Britain against a foreigner, the hated French who was ravaging the shores of the world and winning victory after bloody victory under her hero Bonaparte. Nothing mattered to me now, except that I should serve this magnificent captain and blow the Frenchies out of the sea. Now less than fifty yards separated the two men o' war. And the air was filled with the whine of grape-shot and shriek of canister, and, like a bass drum to this orchestra of death, the ten and twenty-four pounder broadsides thundered across the sea between us, smashing men and timber alike.

A pile of dead and wounded men were strewn over the decks as I followed Willie down the starboard gunports: cannon were overturned, men and restrainer ropes and pulleys entangled in a grotesque web of death, the embrasures were smashed, their foot-thick timbers rearing skywards.

'Prepare to board!' came the captain's cry. 'Mr Soper, where the devil are you?'

'Mate's dead, Captain,' shouted a midshipman.

'Right – Bos'n, follow me. Helmsman, bring her round! You've wind enough, man, bring her round for boarding!'

'Wheel's stuck jammed, sir!'

And the moment he said this the *Sea-Hawk* raised high her prow like a bird in flight. The deck slanted. Losing my footing, I fell headlong, and rose, snatching at Willie, who was still trying to serve a gun, aged thirteen. My grasp missed him, and he slid neatly through the torn embrasure into the sea. Up, up went the prow, with cannon and equipment and the shambles of the decks pouring headlong sternwards, and I saw men flinging up their arms before being buried in the avalanche of death. I saw it coming, and flung myself towards the gun the boy was trying to serve; missed my footing, fell, and rose and dived again for the torn embrasure. And the instant I was through it the *Sea-Hawk*, as if lifted by a giant fist, turned vertically, and slid into the sea stern first. Even as I hit the sea, she plunged, and I rose to the surface flinging water from my hair in that moment before she dived to eternity. And in diving she drew us all to her bosom – floating beams, splintered masts, the refuse of the shattered Frenchman, sucking all in a gigantic, roaring whirlpool down to the bed of the ocean. For the first time in my life I was faced with death. Down, down in a headlong rush amid a cobweb of spars and rigging and struggling men, to rise as suddenly in a terrifying uprush of water that lifted me clear of the sea. Automatically, blindly, I struck out, going from wreckage to wreckage; the upturned spars, the batten-boards and scupper-covers and makeshift rafts where men clung limply in the last stages of consciousness. Willie the powder-monkey I saw, lifeless in the sea, and then Tom, his friend, embracing with lifeless arms the empty powder-tin, now buoyant, with which he had served the *Sea-Hawk*'s guns. Mr Soper, I saw; dead at the instant of impact, and flung mutilated where the ball had taken him: Sam O'Shea I passed as I swam laboriously for the distant coast of Bray, and the mate to the Bos'n, whom some called Tiny, because he was six-foot-three. Others I saw whom I recognized, from long-boat or hammock, or serving the guns, but I did not stop for these; nor did I stop for men who called to me, for the mission of my father was again coming alive within me; imperative and strong. And, despite the carnage and stink of it, the doleful cries of the wounded and the dying, the will to survive grew stronger and stronger – not for my own paltry life, but for Ireland.

Last of all, as I swam away from that scene of desolation, I saw the Englishman. Floating and free, he was, with his hair waving like weed, and his eyes closed in death, and, amazingly, he was smiling, and I gave a thought to his wife and child waiting on the road to Lucan. But one lives for the living, not for the dead, and I pushed him aside because he was lying between me and the Bray headland, and beyond the headland was the Black Boar Tavern where Mia, with luck, might still be waiting. I swam swiftly, for a French long-boat was prowling the sea, looking for survivors, and I could hear the foreign shouts and the answering cries of the English.

Impelled by this new threat, I struck out harder, and cried aloud with a sudden and agonizing pain in my left shoulder. Turning on to my left side, I lumbered on, putting all the distance possible between myself and the rescuing Frenchmen, for gallantry was a creed in their navy; they never left men to drown.

Before me, driven by the tide, were some floating scupper-boards and I clung to one of these, gasping for breath, propelling myself wearily by my legs. Distantly, on high surges of the swell, I could see the sands of Bray: the sun burned down in vicious splendour. Over my shoulder I saw the French frigate changing tack for a seaward course, and gave a prayer. Almost helplessly now, with but enough strength left to cling to the scupper, I let the tide swill me inshore. Nearer, nearer came the beach. The sun was overhead as my feet struck the shingle, instantly tripping me into the breakers, and these took me in great, foaming surges over the shingle with the scupper-board cart-wheeling along beside me in the surf.

Later, deep in the dunes, I clutched the St Christopher medallion, and remembered Kathleen Lehane. But I was not the only man to come ashore at Bray that day: scores came after, it was said, and many alive: the dead also came; many prisoners were taken by the French, including Captain Simmonds, I heard later. After hours of rest, I rose from the dunes and staggered along the beach towards Bray. I fell early, I remember; rose and fell again. And cutting through the weariness and pain was a single, repeated demand:

The letter.

The letter.

12 The face in the corpse-candle

I ARRIVED close to the Black Boar Tavern in the afternoon heat and crawled into a ditch beside the road. I must have slept, for when I awoke a thirst was raging in me after swallowing salt water; my lips were parched, my tongue swollen in my mouth. And I knew again the vicious, stinging pain in my left shoulder. Turning on my back, eyes clenched to the sun, I tore back my doublet and shirt, and saw that heaped blood was congealed from shoulder to bicep. Gently, I touched the flesh and cried aloud with pain. Here, in the heat of the sea-battle, a little iron splinter must have taken me, and the touch of it was like the tip of a needle. It was not so much the size of the splinter, but the wound was going septic and my arm was swelling down to the elbow.

Water.

The fever of the wound brought a gasping need for water. Face down in the ditch now, I dreamed of cooling seas of pure white water, cascading over my aching body: through half-closed eyes I saw a mirage of water that seemed to surge in waves down the empty road to Bray. I must have slept longer this time, for when I awoke it was dark. Above me the stars glittered, and the moon, round and full with him, bounded like a hunter in the sky. Dragging myself up, I saw in that darkness a solitary light – Black Boar Tavern. Suddenly, it began to rain: as if in answer to my prayer for water, it rained; softly, very gently at first, then harder; now pouring in sheets that swept over the dark country. I tore off my doublet, allowing the water to run over my aching body. After a few minutes I rose, staggering towards the light where, I hoped, I would find Mia. But, reaching the tavern, a faintness swept over me, numbing my brain. Kneeling below the bay window of the inn, I peered over the sill. The room, where so recently the press-gang had taken me, was now full of men; loyalist militia, by the look of them, drinking deep in bass laughter, and I saw no peasants. Silently, I crept round the building to the stable yard, and there the world spun about me. I fell, dropping into a bottomless pit of unconsciousness.

'*Whisht,* you... !' whispered a voice.

It was a woman's voice that entered my growing consciousness, and I saw her face, misted at first, then in the shadows of a lamp. And as I opened my eyes she clapped her hand across my mouth.

'*Whisht!*' she breathed, her face close to mine.

It was Biddy, the little tap-maid of the Black Boar Tavern.

'Help me,' I said.

'What ye think I'm doin', man?' She flashed a glance over her shoulder and I realized that I was in a stable; that Mia was beside me stamping; that my head was resting on her precious saddle. Biddy said:

'I found ye in the yard, and I thought you were drunk, until I saw the wound on ye, and found the white cockade in your pocket. Me father said ye'd be dead for sure in the battle with the French.'

'Are you with me, girl?' I asked.

'I am, for sure, but me father'd hand ye to the Militia as soon as look at ye. Where are ye bound?'

'Dublin.'

'Ye can't horse it in this state!' She stared at me. 'Your shoulder's got iron in it, don't ye realize that?'

'I have got to get to Dublin. If you love Ireland, woman, you'll help get me to Dublin.'

'Then the splinter in your shoulder comes out.'

'Can you get a surgeon?'

'Ach, there's no need for that. I've a knife and brandy to sear it clean. Have ye the stomach for it, man?'

I stared at her. She was no more than sixteen.

'If you have,' I said.

'Then wait. I'll be back.' She smiled, adding, 'With your lost rapier.'

I laid back, watching her go; a minute, slim figure in her full, black skirt and her hair in tight curls about her head. She looked a child, but she was a woman.

'Bite on that,' she said, coming back, and thrust a cloth between my teeth. And then she bent to me, ran the point of the knife through the flame of the lantern, dipped it in brandy. And under her hands I nearly died with pain, my teeth clenched. But the iron splinter was out in a gush of poison. She bandaged me, she tipped the brandy to my lips and bid me sleep.

'They will kill you for this,' I said, buckling on my rapier.

'If they do,' she said, 'remember Biddy. The moment

I saw ye I knew you were on important business. Is it to free the country?'

'It is the white cockade,' I said. 'Soon we'll turn it into a green one.'

'God bless ye, and grant ye speed,' she said to me. 'For on one hand we have the likes of you in service to the beloved land, and on the other we've got men such as Jonah Barrington going hell for leather to Dublin to inform on the patriots.'

'Wait,' I whispered, 'what do you know of Jonah Barrington?'

'You saw him yeself, man – he was in the Black Boar on the night the press-gang took ye. And my man Billie Tamber missing him by a whisper between here and Bargy.'

'Your man, eh?' I gave her a grin.

'Ach, sort of, though we're not betrothed. But he's a United Irishman, the same as me, an' that's good measure. The North Cork burned his pa's cabin because, like me, he's a patriot.'

Realisation came to me, and I asked, 'And your Billie Tamber has been tracking Jonah Barrington from Bargy Castle, the home of Bagenal Harvey?'

'He has that. But he's not the brightest in the top storey, if ye get me. He hooked on to the wrong fella south of Carnew – thinking it was Barrington – and got his eye filled up for his trouble.' She pulled at the bandage with strong hands. I said with a chuckle:

'It was me filled his eye up, but he's a fine patriot man, for all his stupidity.'

'Is that a fact!' She flung back her head, stifling her laughter, then whispered:

'But he's nobody's fool, and Barrington's not far ahead . . .'

'Much too far – he'll be in Dublin by now, woman.'

I rose unsteadily.

'May God preserve ye,' she whispered. 'You have the prayers of Biddy O'Keefe,' and she crossed herself, adding, 'Now away wi' you, for soon the Militia will be out. Here, take this,' and she gave me a packet of food and a bottle of wine. She helped me on to Mia's back and led me down a lane away from the Black Boar Tavern. And as I galloped along the road verge for Dublin I looked back but once, seeing her arm raised in farewell; my friend of the white cockade in the midst of Ireland's enemies; the sweetheart of the patriot I had fought near Carnew.

Two weeks later the Black Boar Tavern was burned, they told me. And the Militia came and took Biddy O'Keefe for being a rebel.

I reached the outskirts of Dun Laoghaire as a village clock struck in the first red streaks of dawn. Here, feeling stronger and refreshed despite the pain of my wound, I entered a wood and walked Mia through it: most beautiful was that place with the red light shafting the trees and the refuse of countless autumns beneath our feet. Here I reined in and dismounted, and went full length in the leaves, and at that moment Mia screamed and screamed again, rearing up at a strange, red terror.

A corpse-candle was moving slowly through the trees towards us.

Leaping up, I gripped Mia's bridle, whispering to her, soothing her panic.

And, together, we watched this omen of death by fire.

In bog-land and peat-land the corpse-candles move. The issuing gas ignites by some strange chemistry, and the little pillar of fire moves over the land, three feet high, mostly, withering and dancing in weird shapes and colours, and to see one means a rendezvous with death. Rooted, I stared as it approached us, and Mia, in a frenzy of fear, shrieked and shrieked as something being mutilated, until the flame died slowly at my very feet. Smoke rolled up.

And in that rolling smoke, through some unknown fever of the brain, I saw a vision.

It was the agonised face of a man enduring the torture of the pitch cap, horrifying in its grimaces.

Coughing, I leaped across Mia's back and we went through that wood like things scalded, and we did not stop until we reached the Dublin road. There we took to high ground. On the topmost crag I reined in, staring back along the road to Bray. Pale light flashed on stirrups and bridle; faintly came the echo of hooves. And, even as I watched, the echoing ceased.

I was not the least surprised.

The man who had followed me from the moment I had left the *Rouen* at Carnsore Point in Wexford, was using me to lead him to the hiding-place of Lord Edward Fitzgerald. At last I realized it; at last I knew.

Within a few miles west of Dublin city I crossed the road to Lucan, and to my astonishment I had still not run into patrols of militia or dragoons. But they were burning peasant cabins right enough, for I could see the plumes of smoke in the sky, and for this reason took across country. In a little lane I overtook a woman carrying a child: footsore and weary was she though dressed in silk and finery, and grief was in her face. And she turned to me as I came abreast of her and said:

'Help me, in the name of God.'

Dismounting, I approached her, and she asked, with tears in her eyes, 'Sir, is this the road to Lucan?'

'It is, ma'am,' I replied, and bowed to her.

She held the baby against her, saying, 'The soldiers are burning the cabins of the peasants and digging for hidden arms. Many times they have stopped and searched me.'

'Where have you come from?'

She answered, saying, 'My husband and I were coaching up from Waterford, to begin a new life with his parents, farming in Lucan, but the press-gang stopped the coach outside Bray and took him by force, also the driver. Later the soldiers came and took the horse for a wagon.'

'You are English?'

She nodded. 'My husband's people also, and I would to God we were back in England. How far is it to Lucan?'

I knew, then, that fate had brought me to the wife of the Englishman who had been killed aboard the *Sea-Hawk*. I knew, also, what God expected of me. I said, 'It is about five miles to Lucan, but it will seem that much shorter aboard this mare.'

'You will take us?' Bright and wonderful was her smile. 'My husband will repay you for such kindness!'

'I cannot take you, ma'am, but Mia will, and welcome. All I ask is that you feed and keep her safe until I come for her in Lucan. Can ye ride, lady?'

'I was born in a saddle,' said she, smiling.

Turning from her, I took the letter to Lord Fitzgerald from its secret slot and buttoned it in my doublet. Then I helped the lady into the saddle, and Mia rolled a white eye at me and gave me a look to kill at this indignity, for she did not like women.

'Why are you doing this for me?' asked the lady, smiling down.

I said, 'Because of a man I once knew. Unless I am mistaken, he would have done the same for me.'

I bowed deep to her as she took down the lane to Lucan.

And the moment she had rounded a bend and out of sight, I leaped into the undergrowth at the side of the road, drew the rapier, and waited.

I had come too far and suffered too much to fail my father now.

When I was younger and under instruction in the Academy of Duelling in Paris, it was considered murder if you killed an opponent when once you had achieved a certain standard of training.

Now, however, such gallantry would have to be forgotten.

I intended to kill the man who was following me, for too much was at stake.

The life of Lord Edward Fitzgerald could be endangered if I allowed this tracking to continue. So I waited, tense and ready, for my pursuer.

Only one of us, I decided, would be going to Dublin.

13 The men of the blazing cap

HIDDEN in the undergrowth along the lane to Lucan I waited until the sun was overhead, and still the horseman did not come. And it appeared to me, lying there in ambush that he was attached to me by an invisible string: that when I moved so he moved: that some strange sixth sense bade him stop when I stopped. Now I rose from the ditch after eating and drinking some of the wine Biddy O'Keefe had given me, and made across the bog-land in the direction of Dublin. Strength was flooding back into me, for the poison had gone from my left shoulder and only the ache of the wound remained. And distantly, from the top of a mount, I could see the ragged outline of Dublin city in the coming dusk. Earlier, I had stood for the Angelus, and in the distant pealing of the bell, had known my God.

With the spires of Dublin now in sight, I knew that He was beside me, as always.

With confidence renewed, I strode on, breaking at times into a run as my goal came nearer, and the lanes narrowed into cart-tracks into a forest clearing, and here I rested before the last journey into the city, believing that at last I had lost my pursuer. The moon was rising in a sky of gold, and I drew the letter from my pocket and held the envelope up to the pale light, reading the city address for the first time:

Lord Edward Fitzgerald,
(*care of* Mr Murphy, at the home of the Moore family.)
Thomas Street, Dublin.

Note this: If unable to deliver at above address, try the house of Lady Fitzgerald, Moira House, in vicinity of Usher's Island.

Folding the envelope carefully, I placed it in the heel of my boot, a place of concealment a little less obvious than the breast pocket of my leather doublet. Outstretched in leaves, I slept.

I awoke near midnight, and there was a great hush over the world, as if the finger of God was lifted above it, and the evening star was large and glittering blue with him, and Venus making her Sign of the Cross. And through this universe of planets a million gallons of Milky Way flooded the heavens: a night of goodness, I thought, yet, for me at least, it proved a night of evil.

Now, despite my brief sleep, there was a great weariness in me, and I longed for the moment when I would kneel before Lord Edward Fitzgerald, my mission accomplished. I walked slowly through the trees, and the road to Dublin was deserted under the moon. Soon scattered houses grew before me, and I made my way into the suburbs and along cobbled streets where inn signs creaked and leaded windows stared with blind eyes down at the stranger. Dublin was empty of all but sleeping humans: mangy dogs cringed from me along the gutters; cats hissed and spat from ragged walls, and the whole city grew about me in a crazy hotch-potch of leaning gables and crooked chimneys; a town that coffined its dead in a snoring, whistling orchestra of sleep. Nothing moved in this living tomb of the deathless night; my footsteps echoed like a Newgate gaoler's along the little cranked alleys: no lights burned, not a chink came from the curtained windows. It was as if the big May moon had slammed the lid of the coffin called Dublin and screwed it solid into the down-filled earth. Yet, within a few hours, the sun would rise and Dublin would awake to its raucous street-criers, its chattering markets and the shouting challenge of its corner busybodies. Dead as dust now, it would become reborn in all its charm and gaiety, its misery and laughter, its hunger and its tears, and fine ladies under parasols would trip along the cobbles, where I was treading now with an approaching dread.

Now a strange, new dread was seizing me as I went slowly up Watling Street, for I knew my Dublin like the back of my hand: the dread increased now with every step, for deep within me an instinct warned me—that I was walking into a trap. There was no basis for this fear, yet it was enhanced by the very silence of the sleeping city, by the very fullness of the moon in this criss-cross, baying moonbeam of a night. And then, quite suddenly, the sky was blanketed: blackness, a pitch darkness fell over the streets. I stopped, in utter loneliness and spine-chilling fear, and listened.

I heard, in a little sigh of the wind, the bass whisper of a man.

I looked up. Black clouds were rushing over the moon, and in that lonely darkness I backed away to a wall, my hands outspread, my heart pounding. For the first time in my life I knew real and absolute fear: the chilling numbness that freezes the muscles, forbidding movement.

Yet somehow, in this obliterating blackness, I had to find Thomas Street. And then, from the direction of the stables behind Watling Street, came the iron-tipped rasp of a boot: faint whispering, I heard, and sighing. I stiffened, flattening my body into the shadows of the wall, and a hand rasped the brickwork within a yard of me, like the hand of a blind man scours as he feels his way.

Close to me in this merciless blackness of night, a man was breathing.

Behind me; behind the very wall against which I was flattened, I heard the dull tread of measured steps, and the creak of a door. And I knew that although these enemies were invisible to me, they were slowly, inexorably surrounding me, drawing a net about me from which there was no escape.

It was the fear of the unknown that was numbing my senses. Had they been a score of men, in daylight, I could have made a fight of it. But now I shrank from the evil like a man condemned.

I sensed, rather than saw the man standing directly before me. And even as I clenched my good hand for the attack, a match was struck, lighting his face. Momentarily, the darkness was banished: I saw that face in redness and shadow and stared into it with a new and nameless fear.

Bracing myself against the wall, I hooked hard. The face drifted away, then sank under the blow.

'Take him,' came a whisper.

And they rushed from all sides, feeling for me, clubbing me to my knees. In a clatter of boots they came, their fists thudding into me; pulling me down, they pinned me there. Six men held me; it was impossible to move.

'Take him inside,' said a voice.

14 The duel

THEY tied and gagged me; they threw me into a small room, and there was no light save from a tiny window where the first red streaks of dawn filtered over the floor. And with that light I awoke, staring about me: nothing moved; the place was grave-silent, and it seemed to me lying there that I was the only creature alive in Dublin.

I discovered that I was lying in straw, like some forgotten medieval prisoner. And, as the dawn rose and the sun searched the room it reflected into my eyes in brilliant flashes from the straw, dulling my brain as if in some strange self-hypnotism. Gradually, the events of the night flooded into me and I squirmed into a sitting position, my back to the wall: there, with numbed limbs, and still gagged, I watched the dawn flood over the world and heard the city awakening about me. And as the city awoke, so did the house above me, and then I realized that I was in a cellar. Boots clumped on boards; I heard the rough oaths of men, the sound of pails and the clanking of a pump-handle from a yard. Within an hour the door of the cellar opened and a man came in followed by another, and both were Hessians. I recognized them instantly, with their brown uniforms and knee-length boots of black leather, the thick brown belts at their waists that held their poinyards. They were squarely built, powerful men, and one was at least six feet tall; the other, nearly as broad as he was high, was possessed of an evil that came with him into the room. Stooping, the tall man pulled off my gag and cut the ropes that held me.

'Now you eat, eh?' Going outside, he returned with a bowl of oatmeal and a pitcher of water, and waited while I chafed the blood into my swollen fingers, and I could have cried with the pain of the returning circulation. He pushed the bowl against me.

'You eat now, rebel.'

'Good that you eat now, rebel,' said the smaller man.

'We very good soldiers.'

'We feed you good, rebel.'

'Before Captain Labat come to hang you, eh?' The smaller one regarded me, his little piggy eyes bright in his square, fat face, and drew his finger across his throat.

So I was to face Labat. Sweat flushed to my face in my horror. The tall man said:

'Good that you eat, boy. Captain Labat, he ask many questions when he comes – you eat good, is it?'

I swallowed the oatmeal like swallowing chaff, and washed it down with water. I acted as if I could not hear them, for I was weighing the situation. The cellar door was still open and I could see a light shining beyond it. But they were big men, and born to fight: I knew in my heart that I could not handle the pair of them. The soldier said, 'You tell Captain Labat truth, eh?'

'Yes,' I said, wanting to be rid of them.

'You tell him truth, all right. You tell him lie, and he string you up, eh?' The smaller of the two made the action of hanging himself, his tongue out, stamping his feet.

'Or may be get the pitch-cap.'

The big one said, gripping my shoulder, 'You are very young rebel – you tell truth and swear by your Holy Virgin, and Captain Labat will let you free, perhaps?'

'Perhaps,' said the other, and made a fist of his hand and swung it in the air, laughing. 'But in case he needs it, I will make one now.'

The taller soldier broke into a tirade of anger, kicking shut the cellar door; a quarrel ensued that nearly came to blows. I ate slowly, spooning up the oatmeal. The blood was running freely through my limbs again, and I again wondered if I could take the pair of them, but almost immediately the quarrel subsided. The big man went out; the smaller gave me an evil grin, crossed the cellar floor and sat under the window, watching me. From his pocket he took a band of thick brown paper, and this he began meticulously to fold into shape, then measured it about his forehead, nodding sagely. I gave him a cheerful wink, despite the growing terror within me, and his grin faded into a scowl of anger.

This is the dregs of manhood: it was disgusting to have to share the room with him. I wondered, watching him, how many men had screamed under his hands in his ravages of Ireland: if men in high places realized the agony they had unleashed upon a helpless Irish peasantry by letting loose such barbarians as these. Suddenly I saw that he was wearing my rapier, adding insult to his sadistic clowning, and the sight of it infuriated me. I now knew that he had been deliberately sent to terrorize me before the arrival of the fearful Carl Labat.

In this he was succeeding, but of one thing I was sure.

Before they sent me to eternity I would take this one with me, in the holy name of Ireland.

Captain Labat came at midday, as my guard had informed me.

'Today he come from Clontarf, where he is stationed. Tomorrow he will come from Kinsale – he is here, he is there: nobody see him come, no man see him go – not even me, and I have been Hessian soldier for two years.'

He was about to see him now, by the sound of things: from the street came the clash of arms and shouted commands.

'And today he come specially for you,' added the guard.

Now soldiers were tramping outside the cellar; now the door swung open. My guard leaped to attention. Standing alone, I turned from the window.

I stared. My jaw opened in my utter incredulity.

Before me, in the uniform of a Hessian officer, stood Monsieur Poincaré, my father's friend: Monsieur Poincaré of the French Directory; captain of the gallant little *Rouen* who spied on Nelson's fleet in Milford: the man who had ambushed me outside Fishguard to save me from the Hessians, his regiment!

After my astonishment came humour; I could have shouted with laughter.

And after this came relief; I breathed a prayer of thanks.

Poincaré jerked his thumb at the guard, who saluted and left the room instantly, then Poincaré said, whispering:

'John Regan, I beg you to believe this in the name of your father. Carl Labat is dead. I have been following you from Wexford...'

'So it was you following me!' I exclaimed.

'Of course! You would not part with the message. Do you think the French Directory would allow a lad of seventeen to carry, by word of mouth, a message concerning their fleet?'

'A French invasion!'

'Exactly. But you would not allow me to help, so I followed you in order to protect you...'

'And you have killed Labat?'

'Last night, after his men had taken you. I ambushed him on the road to Clontarf, his base. I killed him, and I am wearing his clothes.'

'But the guard – they know him!' I cried.

'The guard do not know him, for they are not regulars. But the Hessians at Clontarf will soon miss him, and come riding here. Now come!'

'I want my weapon – the guard is wearing it.'

For answer he flung open the cellar door, and shouted, 'Guard, give the prisoner back his weapons, and quick!'

The soldier, trembling, momentarily hesitated, and Poincaré gripped him and flung him into the room.

'You fools! You have got the wrong man – give him his weapons!'

Snatching my belt and rapier, I buckled it about me and followed Poincaré into the passage. Here other soldiers sprang to attention while he raved and stormed at them, yelling, 'Every man will remain here until I return!'

White-faced, they stared, and one cried, 'But, Captain Labat, the sergeant gave orders to take him . . .!'

Instantly, he drew his rapier, holding the point at the man's face. 'And he will pay for his life, for he has taken the wrong man! Where is he now?'

'I will fetch him, Captain!'

'You will not! Tell him – just tell him that he will pay with his life in Clontarf for this stupidity!' He went into the street and swung himself into the saddle, and I knew instantly that he was telling the truth: that this was the man who had followed me from Wexford. It was the way he held himself mounted.

But, in the last few seconds, I had learned something more . . .

'A horse, quickly!' he cried now. 'A horse for our comrade!'

A soldier came at a terrified run, leading a little grey mare. Poincaré was already on the gallop as I mounted her and clattered after him, spurring hard. After we were out of sight of the soldiers, he reined instantly, crying:

'Where to, Regan?'

'Follow me,' I replied. Down narrow streets and tortuous alleys we went at a run, scattering people right and left, with top windows coming open and people laying into us with curses and threats.

'You know where Fitzgerald is?' cried Poincaré, riding abreast.

'Moira House,' I replied. 'Follow me!'

The old Moira House to which my father had taken me as a child; the only place in Dublin where I knew Poincaré and I could be alone together.

The gates were open and we clattered into the stable yard, and I dismounted and slammed and barred them. Poincaré also dismounted.

'Well, where is Fitzgerald?' he demanded, looking about him.

'A long way from here,' I said, and drew my rapier. 'On guard, Carl Labat.'

He stared at me. 'You young fool, what are you talking about?'

'On guard,' I repeated, approaching him. 'Draw, man, or I will run you through.'

Fear struck his eyes and he backed away, drawing the rapier.

And he drew it with his right hand, as he had done to the soldiers.

Poincaré, the finest blade in France, fought with the left.

I said, 'Monsieur Poincaré was left-handed, Carl Labat. It is always the little mistakes that hang a man.'

He smiled thinly, retreating before me. 'One thing is sure, Regan, he will never fight again, and neither will your father.'

'So you killed them both!' I circled him, sparing a

thought for Georges Poincaré who had been broken under torture.

And I realized, with a sudden chill, that had I told them on the *Rouen* that I possessed a letter, I would not have left the ship alive, for that letter held the address of Lord Fitzgerald, and this is what Carl Labat wanted.

I took him as fast as I could and he proved to be an elephant with the sword. Carl Labat was excellent at terrorizing helpless peasants and burning their cabins, but with a rapier he was a fool, and he knew it. My father had always taught me never to take a life unless there was no alternative, and I knew, with Carl Labat blundering before me, that Ireland would always be in danger while he was still alive. Feinting, I opened his guard and, as he staggered back, I ran him through: instantly he died. Trembling now, I sheathed the rapier.

The servants of Moira House were collecting in anguished stares as he fell. There was no time to explain. Mounting the little mare I galloped for Usher's Island: reaching it, I dismounted and left her to wander, and went the rest of the way on foot.

Thomas Street was deserted of people as I stood in the shadow of a doorway and took from my boot the letter for Lord Edward Fitzgerald.

On the step of the Moore house I knocked and waited, and a servant-girl opened the door.

'I wish to see Lord Edward Fitzgerald, please,' I said to her.

She was young, her eyes bright: amazingly like Kathleen Lehane of Enniscorthy, and the colour left her cheeks, I noticed. She replied, 'You have come to the wrong house, sir. Lord Fitzgerald does not live here.'

'Then may I speak to Mr Murphy?' I took from beneath the lapel of my doublet the white cockade, and this I gave to her. 'Please give this to Mr Murphy and tell him that I am a messenger from Milford.'

'Wait here,' she instantly replied, and curtseyed.

I stood waiting: footsteps I heard within the house; faint, swift commands were given. In a short while the girl came back.

She led me to a little room; standing within it was Lord Fitzgerald.

He was tall and handsome; there was a marvellous dignity about him, in the way he carried himself; aloofness was in him, too, which comes with the aristocrat, yet his manner was kind. I said, standing to attention:

'This letter I bring, sir, from Shaun Regan, my father.'

He took the envelope, ripped it, and read the letter, his face expressionless.

'Excellent,' said he, 'I have been expecting this news.' He put the letter into his pocket. 'Your father has been killed, I understand.'

'Yes, sir.'

'Accept my regrets, John Regan. Be honoured that he died for Ireland.'

I did not reply to this, so he said, 'Luckily for me, this letter has arrived in time to give me a warning, yet it is three days late. Did you not have an easy journey?'

Patrick O'Toole and Biddy O'Keefe had given their lives for me. I had been attacked by Billie Tamber, the

Irish patriot, press-ganged, pursued by dragoons, captured by the fearless Hessians and fought and killed Captain Carl Labat.

'Easy enough, sir,' I replied.

'And yet you were late. Do you realize the cost to the United Irishmen? Even before you left Milford Monsieur Poincaré was murdered and his ship, the *Rouen*, captured by the Royalists. My friend Bagenal Harvey of Bargy Castle and nine of his comrades will, by now, have been arrested on the evidence of a man named Jonah Barrington, who came more swiftly than you. The cause is not lost, but it has been endangered because of the time you took to come from Milford to Dublin – a little more than a hundred miles.'

I lowered my eyes before him, and he added:

'Speed is important to us, Regan – your father would have come quicker. Try to do better next time.'

I raised my face to his and saw that he was smiling. 'Yes, sir,' I said.

Strange that I should know of him before he died: proud to death, I was that I should be speaking to a man whose name, I knew, would one day ring in Irish history and be engraved with gratitude on every loyal Irish heart.

And I knew, also, that he would demand nothing of me that he would not give himself.

Come to think of it, five days was a hell of a time to take to get from Milford to the city of Dublin.

Now Lord Fitzgerald turned to the door. 'You have a horse, lad?'

'Yes, my lord.'

'Mia, would that be her name?'

'*Ach*, Mia it is, sir!'

'I know her well. Ride fast, now – do not delay. Ride to Gorey – you know where that is?'

'Outside Enniscorthy, sir.'

'Correct. Ride to Gorey and report there to the parish priest, though his name escapes me. Likewise to this man, be of service.'

Saying this, he then did a strange thing. Taking a backward pace, he bowed low to me.

There's a queer thing to happen, now!

To me, John Regan, who is less than nothing, Lord Fitzgerald bowed.

'Go in God,' he said.

Although it was summer, it was cold in the sunny streets of Dublin, and I walked aimlessly at first, a man in a dream. For as long as I live, I shall never understand why a man as great as that one should bow to a lad as commonplace as me, John Regan.

Still wondering this, I took the road to Lucan to seek out my beloved Mia from the wife of the dead Englishman. After that I must go hell for leather down to Gorey, to find the parish priest, though why this was necessary I did not know, since this was a time of war, not peace.

I could not guess, of course, that the priest to whom I was reporting was the wonderful Father John Murphy: aye, the great Father John who led the rebel army that took Enniscorthy and cut into the redcoats up on Vinegar Hill.

Because the only thing in skirts I had in mind was

one called Kathleen. And, who knows, with a bit of Regan luck I might be walking her over a dream-cloud hill come Sunday, after mass, and not up to my ears in the coming Rebellion.

Remembering Kathleen, I threw strength into my flagging limbs and broke into a run, since the important thing, as Lord Edward Fitzgerald said, was to arrive at places early.

You never know what you might be missing, either, if you keep arriving late.

Historical characters of the 1798 Rebellion

Jonah Barrington

This man, later Sir Jonah Barrington, was a school-fellow of Bagenal Harvey and cousin to Captain Matthew Keugh. Jonah Barrington betrayed Bagenal Harvey, Keugh, and their friends to the Irish Parliament after attending a dinner in Bargy Castle as a guest. All at that dinner were hanged, save Barrington.

Lord Edward Fitzgerald

Younger brother of the Duke of Leinster. Once a member of the Irish Parliament, he served in the American war and was later dismissed from the British Army because of his radical views. Distinguished for his fine character and extreme good looks and noted for his courage as a soldier, Lord Edward became one of the early leaders of the United Irishmen, a society pledged to free Ireland from British rule. This secret society was formed in Belfast in 1791 by a young lawyer, Theobald Wolfe Tone, and his friend Samuel Neilson.

While Wolfe Tone was trying to raise another French expedition to support an Irish rebellion against the British, the 1798 Rebellion broke out, and it was organized and led by Lord Edward. However, the British government, with spies everywhere, knew in advance of the rebels' plans, and struck first. Most of the leaders of the United Irishmen in Ireland were arrested, and among the first to be captured was Lord Edward. He fought bitterly to resist arrest, was mortally wounded, and died some three weeks later. His courage and devotion to his country were above suspicion, his ideals lofty and unselfish. He died for what he considered a sacred cause.

Bagenal Harvey

A Protestant landowner and a man of humane and kindly disposition, Bagenal Harvey was the owner of Bargy Castle (Tomhaggard, near Wexford) at the time of the 1798 Rebellion. Though possessed of great personal courage (he fought several duels), he was not a born leader, and it is thought that he took the leadership more because of popular clamour than for any personal ambitions. He led the rebels in a violent attack on the town of New Ross on 5 June 1798 and at first it appeared certain that they were victorious. But General Johnson, the loyalist commander, counter-attacked while the rebels were celebrating, and drove them from the town. When the rebellion was eventually crushed, Bagenal Harvey, who for so long had striven for moderation and had done all in his power to prevent unnecessary bloodshed, was hanged with other conspirators on the old Wexford Bridge.

Captain Matthew Keugh

Cousin to Jonah Barrington and rebel governor of Wexford at the time of Bagenal Harvey's leadership. A man of great size, good looks and magnetic personality, Keugh did much to prevent rebel excesses and was spoken for by the influential Lord Kingsborough, commander of the infamous North Cork Militia. Like the other rebels, he, too, was hanged on Wexford Bridge. It is said that even in death his good looks did not desert him; that in the horrible exhibition of speared heads, his face maintained the same beauty and quiet resolution that had dignified it in life.

General Lake

This was the General Officer commanding the British and Irish loyalist forces at the time of the 1798 Rebellion. A born soldier, he was inflexible in purpose and merciless in victory. The sixty-five prominent persons hanged on Wexford Bridge were but a small proportion of the vast numbers who died at his command in revenge for the rebellion. Even persons found unarmed in their own houses were slain in cold blood. It is said that after he left Ireland the women and children fled from the sight of a British uniform as from an evil spirit.

McCracken

Leader of the rebel forces which attacked Antrim in June 1798. Henry Joy McCracken was a young Belfast cotton manufacturer and one of the original founders of the United Irishmen whose dream was an independent Ireland. He was a God-fearing man and founded the first Sunday school in Belfast, where, after the failure of the rebellion, he was captured, tried and executed.

Monroe

Henry Monroe was a linen-draper of Lisburn. The rebels selected him as their leader of the insurrection in Down. Success at first attended him, for he drove off the loyalist York Fencibles and yeomanry and cavalry under Colonel Stapelton. But at Porthkerry on 11 June 1798, at the head of some 7,000 rebels, Monroe was repulsed, and later, despite fantastic courage, he was defeated by General Nugent when he attacked Ballinahinch. Henry Monroe was hanged at Lisburn before his own front door, in the presence of his wife and mother. He died bravely and with dignity.

Father John Murphy

This was the Catholic priest who raised the first standard of revolution at Boolavogue, a hamlet on the road between Wexford and Gorey, on 26 May 1798. A statue to Father John can be seen today in the square of Enniscorthy. He is described by one set of historians as ignorant – a narrow-minded fanatic; by others he is depicted as a simple-minded son of the priesthood who was driven to desperation by the burning of his house and chapel by yeomen cavalry. He rapidly took Oulart, Camolin and Ferns with a half-starved rebel army armed mainly with pikes. Following these successes he captured Enniscorthy after a big battle, and camped on Vinegar Hill above the town. On 30 May, driving all before him, he took Wexford itself. But the loyalists who supported the British Crown began to organize, and British troops were shipped into Ireland in vast numbers. After further successes came defeat. Father John, with hundreds of others, many of them priests, was executed. He left behind him a legend. His followers believed he was possessed of supernatural powers, that he could catch bullets with his fingers. His death broke the myth of his believed invincibility.

Wolfe Tone

One of the greatest names of Irish history, Theobald Wolfe Tone, a United Irishman, was in France serving under Napoleon in the French army when the 1798 Rebellion broke out under Lord Edward Fitzgerald. Earlier, in 1796, Tone managed to persuade the French Director in Paris to send an invasion fleet to Ireland to support an earlier rebellion. On 15 December 1796 this fleet set sail from Brest with 15,000 men, seventeen large warships and thirteen frigates. Had this great fleet landed in Ireland, it undoubtedly would have changed the course of Irish history, for the peasants were seething under the cruelty of English rule. However, tempestuous weather was encountered and, broken and battered, the invaders struggled back to Brest.

This was a serious set-back in Wolfe Tone's plans. But in August 1798, as a result of his further endeavours, Napoleon sent another invasion force to Ireland under General Humbert. It was a small force but it managed to land immediately and defeated a British force twice its size. But the rebellion under Lord Edward Fitzgerald was now broken and ended, Ireland was full of British troops, and the French general soon had to surrender. Wolfe Tone persuaded yet another force of Frenchmen to attempt an invasion of Ireland two months later, and sailed with this fleet himself. But the French were attacked by a British squadron and were defeated. Tone was taken prisoner, conveyed to Dublin and there tried and sentenced to be hanged. He asked for a soldier's death by shooting; this was refused, so he committed suicide in November 1798 with a tiny knife he managed to obtain.

Mention is made of Oliver Bond, O'Connor, Sweetman, McCormick, McNevin, Drennan and Lawless. These were all United Irishmen prominent in the fight for Irish independence.

Mention is made of yeomanry and militia. These were mainly Irish by nationality; local regiments composed of farmers and the sons and employees of landowners who supported the British Crown and who assisted British troops in opposing the demands of the United Irishmen and in putting down the peasantry. Of these Irish forces the North Cork Militia under Lord Kingsborough was the most hated and feared, and their treatment of the peasants was largely responsible for the viciousness of the rebel revenge.

The French Revolution and the 1798 Irish Rebellion had common aims. Whereas the former was a revolution against the cruelty and oppression of the aristocracy, the latter was an attempt by Ireland to throw off the yoke and tyranny of British rule which was supporting a system which enriched the landlords and impoverished the peasants.